SEA STORIES

TWENTY-FIVE YEARS IN SUBMARINES

John H. Maurer, Jr.

Captain, USN (Ret.)

Dedication

To Carol, my current girlfriend.

Table of Contents

Introduction

Sea stories. Every sailor has them. Little anecdotes that relate special memories. Some are humorous; some are exciting. Some recall a person worth remembering; some recall an event that we cannot forget. All of them are special, in some way, to the sailor who saves them.

They open conversations. "Remember when ...?" They come up over a beer and pretzels. Some are competitive. "Can you top this ....?" Almost always they are unique to the story-teller, and almost always they are truthful, or mostly so. They usually put the teller in a good light.

These stories are no different. They represent events I participated in and people I knew over three decades and in five submarines, with a couple of shore-side stories thrown in for good measure. They are not connected. There is no thread running through them, and I have not tried to include a theme. Each is to be enjoyed, maybe even believed, on its own merits.

I have worked from memory. No notes or references, so the facts may be shaky. Any dialogue, of course, is reconstructed years after the words were actually spoken. Although the flavor of a conversation is as accurate as I can make it, the exact words were probably a little different.

Classified material has been scrupulously avoided. I do not think I have included any material that could jeopardize national security. It's a shame: some stories would really catch your attention: "Try and top this ...!" To that end, some details have been omitted and some have been disguised. None of these changes (and there are not many) affects the telling of the story.

I have not included discussions of my mistakes (and I've made some doozies). Maybe the memory erases these, or maybe I'm just avoiding painful recollections.

Some of the tales are technical. Mine has been a technical business. Submarines are marvelous machines, and the equipment and systems they comprise are complex and sophisticated. I have tried to simplify the discussions when it will not detract from the story, and I have occasionally suggested that the reader can skip ahead when the going gets a little difficult. For the most part, the details are rigorously correct, if a little allowance is made for narrative convenience (and a fuzzy memory!).

These stories have been written down primarily for my family, so that they can share the events and people that have been so memorable to me. I hope you enjoy them also.

Professional Paths

Tough love

In the summer of 1961, as a first class midshipman, I was assigned to a submarine in Norfolk, the **USS CUBERA**, for my summer cruise. At the time, my parents were also in Norfolk, where Dad was Chief of Staff for the Commander of Atlantic Fleet Submarines (ComSubLant), Admiral Elton Grenfell. Being able to come home at night, when the ship was not at sea, was an added benefit.

The **CUBERA** was scheduled for routine maintenance, and we took the ship into drydock at the Norfolk Naval Shipyard. After the maintenance was complete, we prepared to flood the dock. I was assigned "tank diving" duties in the main ballast tanks.

(A "tank dive" is an inspection tour to ensure that no debris or tools have been left in the tank, which is not easily accessible after the drydock is flooded. Such items can cause rattles when the ship returns to sea, and noise interferes with the ship's sonar.)

In the Norfolk summer, in the ballast tank of a black submarine hull in drydock, with no ventilation, it was HOT. As the junior man in the wardroom, tank diving fell to me, so I set off into the drydock and climbed up into the first (of several) main ballast tanks.

I learned later that Dad had appointments in the shipyard that day, and he concluded them just before lunch. Cool iced tea and lunch at the Officers' Club were definite possibilities. In his white uniform, with all the gold regalia of the Submarine Force Chief of Staff, he walked up to the brow of the **CUBERA**. The Duty Officer hurried topside to meet him.

"Is Midshipman Maurer here?" Dad asked.

"Yes, Sir. He's making an inspection tour of MBT 3A. Just a moment – I'll get him."

"No. Leave him there. It's good for him." And Dad walked back down the brow.

The Flooding Drill

Usurping the Captain's prerogative

It was the summer of 1964, and I had just reported to my first ship. The **USS SCAMP** was commanded by Commander A.J.M. "Tommy" Atkins, USN, a truly extraordinary submariner that I was proud to serve under. (I recognize that many submariners think highly of their first commanding officer, but Tommy Atkins was exceptional. Read on, and you'll see one aspect of his character.)

SCAMP had been my first choice at Submarine School, and my class standing had supported my selection. Even so, I felt that I was fortunate to be aboard. I was not yet qualified in submarines, and I could not wear the gold dolphin insignia. My training was well underway, however, and I knew that the day would eventually come.

Part of my training involved my response to shipboard emergencies, and one day I found myself as the diving officer under instruction. It did not take a genius to realize that some kind of a drill was coming. Sure enough, we heard a noise from forward, followed shortly by a report over the announcing system, "Flooding in the Torpedo Room!" Everyone waited for me to order a response.

I turned to the Chief of the Watch at the ballast control panel and ordered, "Blow the forward group." This order would send high-pressure air into the forward main ballast tanks, and start the ship toward the surface. The Chief looked at me, incredulous, and didn't make a move.

"Blow the forward group, NOW", I yelled, and the Chief opened the valves.

"Secure the air. *I* surface this ship," came an all too recognizable voice from somewhere behind me.

The blow was stopped, the ballast tank vents were opened, and the drill was terminated. I turned the dive over to the qualified diving officer and left the control room.

A brief historical note is in order. I mentioned that it was 1964. The previous fall, the **USS Thresher** had been lost with all hands off Boston. The Submarine Force was determined to learn everything possible from this tragedy. One lesson was that the flooding recovery procedures developed during World War II were not appropriate for the faster, deeper diving submarines we now employed. It was no longer sufficient for a diving officer to "reach and maintain ordered depth." To this was added an emergency response: "<u>Act now</u>. We'll talk about it on the surface."

Specifically, we now recognized that it was vitally important to head for the surface <u>immediately</u>. This used any existing momentum to drive the boat upwards, and the reduced water pressure at shallower depths slowed the inrushing water. *Seconds* counted. This new emphasis on immediate action was being developed and taught at the Submarine School in Connecticut, but it had not yet reached the fleet. Shipboard procedures were still directed toward combating the casualty, restoring depth control and maintaining ordered depth.

Captain Atkins called me into his stateroom later that afternoon and asked why I had elected to usurp one of his most fundamental prerogatives – to surface the ship. His manner was pleasant and professional. This was not a "chewing out" session, but an earnest effort to find out what had gone through my head. I explained the lessons that we had been taught as a result of the **THRESHER** investigation. I acknowledged that I was not familiar with the written **SCAMP** procedure (*I should have been!*) and my actions in the drill "seemed like the thing to do at the time."

We discussed the philosophy behind the new procedures at length, and Captain Atkins listened thoughtfully. When we finished, the Captain emphasized the importance of following written procedures and the equal importance of revising them promptly when new information came to light.

SCAMP was one of the first submarines to formally instate the revised flooding response.

Submarine Mess at Mare Island

The Chief

After graduation from the Academy, Nuclear Power School, and Submarine School, I was ordered to **USS SCAMP** in San Diego. It was 1963. (Yes, we had submarines back then.) My first assignment was as Assistant Operations Officer. "Watch and learn. Help when you can. Stay out of the way."

A few months after I reported aboard, **SCAMP** entered Mare Island Naval Shipyard for a scheduled overhaul. It was time for me to pull my own weight in the wardroom. I became the Supply Officer. Supply was an important but unglamorous job. On small ships, it included Food Service Officer, an even more unglamorous position. In a shipyard overhaul, with the ship's galley and mess hall torn up, it was worse.

At Mare Island, where the shipyard would be overhauling several submarines at a time, the Submarine Force had found an imaginative way to feed the crews:

Each of the submarines would temporarily assign all their cooks to one boat. They would "sell" all their food to that boat. Every month, each submarine would administratively transfer all their "rations" (a "head count") to the chosen boat. The lucky boat would operate a special mess hall on the shipyard for three months, using the ration counts to "buy" foodstuffs. At the end of the quarter, the "duty" would rotate to another submarine. It was a good solution but a real chore if you were the chosen one.

I was fortunate. My Chief Cook had run the Mare Island Submarine Mess, earlier, when he was on another boat. He knew the ropes. I suppose I made some decisions, but I don't remember any. I *do* know that anytime the Chief came to me with a request or suggestion, the correct answer was, "Yes." I never regretted any response.

With many cooks, and a big kitchen, Chief Wally Press was in his element. A cook who liked to bake could now bake, full time. A cook who enjoyed butchery could carve up sides of beef, full time. The economies of scale became apparent. Being able to buy in large quantities (like half a cow) really paid off. We bought the best, and we still couldn't spend all the money the combined ration count allowed. Shipyard sailors who could eat free at the shipyard mess would *buy* their lunch from us. Before long, I was *turning in* extra money every month. (Unheard of!)

I learned another lesson from Chief Press. We bought most of our food from a Naval facility in Oakland, about thirty miles away. We had to call our order in, several times a week. In those days, there were only a few government telephone lines from the shipyard. You called a switchboard operator, and she put your name in a queue. Sometime later, when a line became available, she'd call you back and put your call through. (Prehistoric, right?)

When Chief Press took over the Mess, and periodically thereafter, he baked a delicious cake and sent it over to the switchboard operators. No strings attached. Forever after, whenever Chief Press wanted to call Oakland, a line was somehow instantly available.

We served our three months, and volunteered to keep the Mess for another quarter (also unheard of!) on the condition that our "turn" would not come up again. The Mess was running smoothly, and that was unlikely to change, so the Flotilla Commander accepted our offer.

Chief Press is in Heaven now, running the Angels' Mess. Rumor has it that God is pleased with his performance.

Overload

An encounter with the KOG (Kindly Old Gentleman)

In the summer of 1967, Admiral Rickover was selecting the original crew for **SUBMARINE NR-1**, and I was ordered to fly from San Diego to Washington to be interviewed. I had never heard of **NR-1**, and I was not looking forward to another meeting with the Admiral.

When I was ushered into his office, I was caught by surprise.

"Why did you lie to me?" he asked, without preamble.

Somewhat shaken, I replied, "I have never lied to you, Admiral."

Angry, or apparently angry, Admiral Rickover referred back to my nuclear power program application interview six years earlier. "You told me you would take two overload courses your first class year, and you only took one. Why did you lie to me?"

(The overload program at the Naval Academy involved extra, non-credit courses that midshipmen could take in their spare (!) time. I had been taking additional mathematics courses since my youngster (sophomore) year.)

Now I was on firmer ground. "Sir, I *did* take two overload courses first class year." And I named the courses: "Complex Variables during the first semester and Laplace Transforms during the second."

Now the Admiral was really mad. "No, no! You said you would take *two* overload courses the *second* semester. Why didn't you?"

(I recalled later that many of my classmates had been required to sign up for a double overload burden after our initial interviews years earlier. At that time, the Admiral had been so busy chewing me out for my reliance on my Dad's service reputation that he forgot to demand two second semester overload courses, and I was not about to volunteer. (That "reliance" is discussed in another story in these pages.). My classmates were amazed and envious when we compared stories on the bus ride back to Annapolis.)

I held my ground. "Admiral, I *never* promised you that I would take two overload courses during the second semester of first class year."

During any personnel interview, Admiral Rickover would always have an officer seated near the door to take notes on the questions and responses. We were all familiar with this procedure. He had one now, just as he had six years earlier.

"Why do you think I keep a record of every interview?" he asked.

This one was easy. "Sir. So that you can accurately reproduce the results later."

The Admiral picked up a paper on his desk, waved it at me, and roared, "If this piece of paper says you agreed to take two overloads, and you tell me you only agreed to take one, who am I supposed to believe?"

I answered, "You should believe me, Admiral."

"GET OUT!" and to the officer who was taking notes, "And get me the results of his initial interview!"

I spent two hours in the "penalty box", and I was then taken back in to see the Admiral. Overload courses were never mentioned. The Admiral was pleasant and conversational. He explained the importance of **NR-1**, and he asked if I wanted the job. By this time, I knew more about the ship, and I answered, "Yes." Admiral Rickover said he would make his decision and let me know. The interview was over, and I returned to San Diego.

Three days later, I was told that my next duty station would be **NR-1.**

Called to Washington

People are often not what we think

There were three officers in the original crew of **SUBMARINE NR-1**. Dwaine Griffith was the Officer in Charge, Steve Perry was the Engineer, and I was "everything else". In practice, Steve oversaw the construction of the reactor plant and I watched the "front end." Dwaine, of course, was responsible for the whole ship.

Both Dwaine and Steve had frequent interactions with the Naval Reactors staff, and so we were surprised to hear, one day, that Admiral Rickover wanted *me* to come to Washington. Why me? Was the Admiral interested in some aspect of the ship's oceanographic suite? Should I prepare something for him to review? Perhaps I had screwed up somehow, and the Admiral wanted to "discuss" my error with me.

Dwaine tried to get answers, but he was not successful, though he was reassured that there was no problem. "Just tell Maurer to come, and not to worry," was the only response he received from Admiral Rickover's staff.

At the time, Dad was the Commander of the Pacific Fleet Submarine Force (ComSubPac) at Pearl Harbor. Although I did not realize it, he was flying to Washington for discussions at the Pentagon. At any rate, I boarded a plane to Washington and took a cab to Admiral Rickover's offices on the Mall. I was met by our Project Manager, Tip Brolin.

"You're probably wondering why you're here", said Tip.

"The question had crossed my mind", I answered.

Tip handed me my ticket back to Connecticut for later that evening, and said, "Your Father is here from Honolulu, and the Admiral thought you might like to have lunch with him."

I never saw the Admiral that day, and I had a most enjoyable lunch with Dad. I have enjoyed relating this story whenever anyone has said that Admiral Rickover didn't care about his people.

The Wet Suitcase

A design error - corrected

Near the end of the construction phase at Electric Boat Company, we found ourselves more and more involved in testing new equipment. One night, the Sperry engineers brought down our new bridge suitcase. The suitcase was a portable, water-resistant case, about twelve by eighteen inches, and about eight inches deep. It contained a communication microphone and speaker, alarm switches, and a gyrocompass repeater that could be lifted out and mounted on the edge of the sail. The suitcase provided essential connectivity between the Officer of the Deck on the bridge and the helmsman below-decks when the ship was proceeding on the surface.

On the evening in question, Fred DeGrooth and Roger Sherman, the Sperry field engineers who had been involved with **NR-1** from the beginning, carried the suitcase to the bridge and began to energize its various circuits. A light rain, more like a mist, was falling, and the engineers spread a piece of polypropylene sheeting over the suitcase to keep it dry.

A bucket of sea water was sitting on the ship's deck near the sail. I picked up the bucket, pulled the waterproof sheeting off, and dumped the water over the suitcase.

As expected, sparks flew and breakers popped open as the circuits were grounded by the salt water. The suitcase was thoroughly "fried."

The Sperry corporate office was incensed (Fred and Roger just laughed), and I was asked, "How much water went onto the suitcase?"

I estimated, "About a tenth of a wave."

The point was made, and the suitcase was redesigned to be waterproof.

Plush or Berber?

A new kind of sound absorbent material

The Electric Boat Company was in a bind. The shipbuilding contract for **SUBMARINE NR-1** included, by reference, the U.S. Navy's "General Specifications for Building Ships." These requirements covered everything from lighting to lifelines. Shipbuilders were familiar with these specifications, and they had long since incorporated them in their designs and procedures. Compliance was guaranteed by a formal testing program, and the prospective crew of a ship being built had to agree that a given requirement had been met satisfactorily.

We on the **NR-1** crew had long been lobbying for the provision of carpet on the ship's deck forward of the engine room. It would add a nice touch to our otherwise Spartan living conditions. But such carpeting was not included in the building specifications, general or otherwise, and we were politely told to pound sand.

One of the "General Specifications" addressed ambient noise in ship's operating spaces. Obviously, it would not do to have loud machinery in spaces where people needed to be able to communicate. One evening, the shipbuilder's test personnel arrived with sound level instrumentation, and announced that they had come to verify compliance with the noise specification. **NR-1** had little machinery outside of the engine room, and the engineers anticipated few problems. They set up their instrumentation and prepared to record our sound levels.

What these engineers did not realize, is that the operating philosophy for **NR-1** specified that our search sonars would be turned *on*, and their speakers would be playing in the background. When a contact returned a signal, the musical chirp would be heard by the pilot, and he would call for assistance. The ambient noise level test was required to be run in the ship's "normal operating condition" and this was our "normal".

I went around the space, turning *on* all the sonar speakers, and of course we failed the test miserably. We, the ship's company, would not approve the test results as "satisfactory".

Several days later, at a regular **NR-1** progress conference, the subject of the ambient noise test arose. The shipbuilder's hands were tied. The contract required him to meet an impossible specification. The Naval Sea Systems representative (NavSea was the "customer") was understandably reluctant to propose (to Admiral Rickover, among others) that a waiver of the Navy's general shipbuilding specifications was required for **NR-1**. And we, on the ship, could obviously not accept a test that had failed.

Stalemate.

After comments bounced back and forth, I proposed that sound-absorbent material be installed on the plane surfaces in the compartment. There appeared to be no other way. The shipbuilder's representatives grimaced, having visions of the difficulties they would face trying to build sound-absorbing covers for dozens of installations.

"Of course", I said, "the largest plane surface in the space is the deck. And carpet absorbs sound pretty well ...."

The carpet was installed, and the test re-run. The test still failed, but we accepted it with an asterisk that probably never saw the light of day. Everyone was happy: the shipbuilder's test program was intact, the NavSea representative did not have to face the Admiral, and we got our carpet.

We even got to choose the color.

A Broken Wire

Healing a broken arm

Sometimes, a problem appears unsolvable because of its location. A failure <u>outside</u> the pressure hull of a submarine is a good example. The solution, however, may be far away from the problem, and if that solution happens to be inside the submarine, so much the better.

SUBMARINE NR-1 had an external arm, or manipulator, for use in recovery of artifacts from the ocean floor. When not in use, the manipulator was folded up and stored in the submarine's box keel. The entire structure was outside the pressure hull, and so it was not accessible at sea.

The manipulator arm was hydraulically operated and it had six "joints" (elbow, shoulder, wrist, etc). Each joint had an installed servo valve that controlled its movement (up-down, left-right, extend-retract, etc.). Hoses supplied the hydraulic fluid. A multi-circuit underwater cable carried the control power to an external junction box, from which the proper circuit was routed to each servo valve.

This section gets a little technical, so you can skip ahead to the next paragraph if your eyes start to glaze over. Each servo valve had three connections: a plus (6 volts), a minus (-6 volts), and a variable. Each valve had two windings that controlled how the valve ported the oil ("up" or "down", etc.). Normally, the two windings opposed and balanced each other, and the joint stayed where it was. When you wanted to move a joint, the "variable" connection was used to change the voltage at the point between the two windings. Then, one winding pushed harder, and the other (opposed) winding eased up. The valve ported the oil in the chosen direction, and the joint moved.

As we were operating on a mission, with the arm extended and unfolded, disaster struck. The "plus" wire in the cable to the external junction box broke, and we could not move any of the arm's joints. The arm was extended, and (essentially) dead. When we eventually surfaced and started rolling around (as was all too normal!), our $2 million arm would break off and be lost.

We broke out the circuit diagrams and tried to figure a way out of our dilemma. The "minus" wire and the "variable" wires for each joint were still intact. It was only the "plus" power to all the joints that was lost. If we could find a way to send current out to a joint control valve, even though we would only reach one of the two valve windings, we might have a chance.

Having the circuit diagrams was a crucial piece of good fortune. We located a connector that was inside the submarine and was the "inside end" of the cable with the broken wire. We were able to identify the pins that represented the "minus" wire and the "variable" wire for each joint. We connected a lantern battery and a variable resistor box (normally used for reactor instrumentation calibration) in series, and fed the tiny current to each valve in turn. By gradually reducing the setting on the resistor box, we could slowly increase the current.

We had one person watch the manipulator through the viewport. When a joint started to move in response to the increased current, he could tell if the joint was moving in the correct direction – toward the "stowed" position. If the joint started moving in the wrong direction, we simply reversed our connection to the pins at the connector.

We were able to move each joint, in turn, to the proper "stowed" position, and we retracted the arm back into the keel. We turned off the hydraulics, put everything away, and continued our mission.

Easy now ... easy ... LIFT!

SUBMARINE NR-1 was at home on the ocean bottom. We could see out the three viewports near the bow, and the area near the ship was illuminated by a battery of lights. Television cameras covered spots that could not be seen from the viewports. Sonar equipment reached out into the darkness to give us an idea of what lay outside our fields of vision.[1]

Two large truck tires (filled with incompressible alcohol) could be lowered from the box keel beneath us, and the main propulsion motors could move us ahead comfortably. Our thrusters could turn us right or left. A navigation system, using a variety of inputs, could keep track of our position, and its charts could suggest where we should go next, when we were searching for something, which was often our mission.

When we found and came up to our objective, a hydraulic arm (the "manipulator") could be used to pick up the object, and we could place it a basket assembly that was accessible when we returned to the surface. The manipulator, however, was limited in the weight it could lift. Sometimes, we needed to move assemblies that were heavier than the manipulator's capability.

We solved this problem with a little ingenuity. One of our Machinists Mates, Glenn Seaton, welded together a treble hook not

---

[1] One of the original nine crewmen of SUBMARINE NR-1, Lee Vyborny, has written an excellent book about the boat. I read DARK WATERS, AN INSIDER'S ACCOUNT OF THE NR-1, THE COLD WAR'S UNDERCOVER NUCLEAR SUB in two days. I couldn't put it down, and I was there! I heartily recommend it.

unlike those found in any fisherman's tackle box (though without the barbs!). The prongs were about eight inches long, and there was always at least one facing you. Petty Officer Seaton attached the hook to the underside of the ship, within reach of the manipulator.[2]

If we knew before a mission that we would have to move something heavy, and we had those objects available to us, we would simply attach a ten-foot pendant to the object. The pendant would have a six-inch eye at the unattached end. In use, we would grab the pendant with the manipulator and loop the eye over a prong of the hook. Then, we could use the entire buoyancy capability of the ship. As we pumped water overboard, the boat would rise and lift the object clear of the bottom. We would then drive to the desired location, ease the boat down until the ocean bottom supported our load, and cast the pendant eye off the hook.

We used a variation of this scheme for the AFAR project in the Azores.[3] For that project, underwater transponders would be used to lower underwater towers to known bottom locations. One of our tasks was to reposition each transponder assembly, after which its location could be precisely surveyed.

For each assembly, a deep-sea transponder was suspended beneath a float, with an anchor block hanging about a hundred feet below the transponder. Each three-piece assembly was lowered over the side of a surface ship, and it would sink a half-mile or so to the ocean bottom.

---

[2] As you might imagine, this has been known forever afterwards as the Seaton Hook!

[3] The AFAR Project was a NATO-sponsored underwater construction project near the Azores Islands. **SUBMARINE NR-1** supplied most of the underwater engineering.

We were to find each assembly, pick it up, and carry it to its proper location.

For this task, we instructed the crew topside to attach a ten-foot pendant to the *top* of each float. As before, the pendant would have an eye at the unattached end. We added a small "peanut" buoy to hold the eye above and clear of the float itself. In use, we grabbed the eye with the manipulator, looped it over one of the hook's prongs, and again used the buoyancy capability of the ship to lift the load. The system worked perfectly. Each transponder assembly was placed in the proper position, the surveys were conducted, and the project towers were lowered to the ocean floor.

It gets better. For one of the assemblies, we could not use the manipulator. (I don't remember why not. Maybe it was out of commission – maybe we were just cocky.) Using the main propulsion motors and the thrusters, we maneuvered the entire ship – 415 tons – to loop a six-inch eye over an eight inch hook. Piece of cake.

The Moving Target

Something's out there, and it may be alive ...

The search sonar on **SUBMARINE NR-1** is a superb piece of electronics. The Straza CTFM (continuous transmission frequency modulated) sonar is properly regarded as the best of its kind. It is installed on all the best deep submergence vehicles. It is reliable and effective, but on one occasion, it scared the dickens out of us.

A proper discussion of this incident relies on an understanding of CTFM principles. Sorry, but you'll have to grit your teeth as I delve into the electronics involved. I'll simplify as much as I can, but ...

The transmitting hydrophone on a CTFM sonar does not put out a "ping" like the one we hear in the movies. Instead it broadcasts a continuous tone that sweeps from a low note to a high note, and then it resets and starts over again. This frequency modulated tone travels out through the water, bounces off a contact, and returns to the receiving hydrophone.

While the tone is traveling out and returning, the transmitter is continuing to sweep up in frequency. If the target is a long distance away, the transmitter will have climbed farther up its frequency sweep by the time the returning signal is received. The outgoing and the returning tones are electronically compared, and the difference between them is displayed as the contact's range,

The contact's bearing is determined by the direction the receiving hydrophone is pointed when it receives the returning tone.

Now comes the fun part, which we only figured out *after* the incident.

In rare instances of extraordinarily fine sonar conditions, the returning tone arrives while an outgoing tone that is <u>two</u> sweeps later is being transmitted. (The returning tone actually leads the outgoing tone, but the electronic comparison circuit can't tell the difference.) Still with me? No matter. Here's the result:

A false blip appears on the display. It looks perfectly real, but its range performance is <u>reversed</u>. As you try to approach the contact, it scoots away. When you back away (as we could on **NR-1**), it moves toward you, like a playful puppy.

We had seen many contacts on our CTFM. We had seen trash cans, oil drums, coffee cans, and rocks too numerous to mention. All of our previous contacts, however, had one thing in common: *they didn't move.* This contact, whatever it was, was different. We finally solved the mystery by simply forging ahead until we could see the contact through a view port.

It was a flat rock, and it didn't move.

Things that Go "Boom" ...

Remnants of a long-ago war

We were crawling along the bottom on SUBMARINE NR-1, searching for a particular target. Our search sonar, the CTFM (continuous transmission frequency modulated, for those who care about such things), could pick up a coffee can at several hundred yards on a flat, sandy bottom[4], and so far, the screen had been blank.

When we received a bright signal, we started to get excited. Because the blip on the sonar display could not show any target details, we had to drive over to the contact for a visual confirmation through the view ports. This was a normal evolution, and it was one we were good at. We didn't give a second thought. We should have.

As we approached the target, another contact appeared in the distance, then a third. We would have to inspect each one, so we had our work cut out for us, but it was better than staring at a blank display. The CTFM seemed to indicate that the contacts were in a straight line. Hmm. That was unusual ...

Before long, we could see the contact through the view port. It was a steel box, cube shaped, about three or four feet on a side. The top was open, and there appeared to be a cable reel and some sort of

---

[4] By the way, the three "laws" of deep submergence operations, of which there are *many* exceptions, are
- We know right where it is.
- Don't worry. We can track you.
- It's a flat, sandy bottom.

mechanism inside. Some wire rope had been pulled off the reel, and it was lying in loops on the sand alongside the box. The end of the wire rope had been cut. This was definitely not our target of interest, so we lifted off the bottom and headed for the second contact.

On the way over, a fourth and then a fifth contact appeared on the screen. These appeared to be in a line that was parallel to the first. Hmm. Curiouser and curiouser ... The second contact was identical to the first, and we again lifted clear to continue our inspection. During our transit, a *third* line of contacts, parallel to the first two, appeared on the screen.

We now knew what they represented. We could picture, years ago, three minelayers steaming along side by side, and deploying mines over the stern. The mines would sink to the bottom, where the anchor assembly (the part we had seen) would release the explosive ball (the mine itself). The mines would rise toward the surface, with the anchor mechanism paying out wire rope from the reel. When a mine reached a set depth below the surface, the anchor mechanism would lock the cable reel, and the mine would begin its patient wait.

After the war, the entire minefield would be "swept". The cables would be cut by sweep gear, and the mines would bob to the surface. There, they would be exploded by rifle fire and the minefield would be declared safe for ships to pass. The loops of wire rope that we observed were the cut ends of the suspension cables.

We still had to inspect each contact. As we approached the third, we noticed that something was different. When this particular assembly sank to the bottom, it did not release its mine, which still nestled menacingly on the top of the anchor. The spherical shape and the detonation "horns" were plainly visible.

Chances are, the mine had not armed, and it was probably inert after years on the bottom, but we were aware of the tragedies that still occur off the coast of France, and we did not want to be proven wrong. We backed away cautiously and left hastily. We closed each remaining contact only enough to verify that it was not our target of interest.

We eventually mapped the entire field, inspecting each contact. About one in every seven mines had failed to deploy, and were still sitting intact on their anchors. None exploded, or this story might have ended differently ...

Tangled on the Bottom

On my wall is a wooden plaque mounting a short length of line and a small brass plate. The engraving reads "SUBMARINE NR-1, November 11, 1970". We probably should have been concerned, but at the time we were simply annoyed.

SUBMARINE NR-1 (like all submarines) was close to neutrally buoyant when we were submerged. Additionally, we had only very limited propulsive power. This combination of low power and near weightlessness meant that even a small line could hold us in place if we somehow became entangled with it. We took this hazard very seriously: Proposals to inspect the sunken liner ANDREA DORIA just south of Long Island were turned down because of the multiple fishing nets which now hung from the ship's masts and superstructure.

For maneuverability near the ocean bottom, NR-1 had four bi-directional thrusters – two forward and two aft. Each pair was mounted in an X configuration. Controlled by a computer linked to the pilot's joystick, the four thrusters could move or twist the boat in almost any direction. We had occasionally drawn a foreign object into a duct and jammed a thruster, which would then promptly overload and pop open its electrical supply breaker.

That is what happened in 1970, but I'm getting ahead of the story…

We had finally convinced our two fine Sperry field engineers to come to sea with us. Fred DeGrooth and Roger Sherman had been with us for more than three years. As far as we were concerned, they were part of the crew. They were soon to be introduced to one of the more unsettling aspects of submarining.

We were on the continental shelf southeast of Long Island, about five hundred feet down. The officer of the deck noted a contact on the search sonar and began to close its position. An observer at the viewports strained to see the contact, but the water was murky and visibility was limited. We were moving in to get a closer look when suddenly, the breaker on one of the forward thrusters popped open and the thruster abruptly stopped.

We could now see the object that had produced the sonar return. It appeared to be a large, metal cage-like structure with several heavy cables extending upward, out of sight, and we began to back clear.

As we backed, the bow dipped toward the bottom, and we abruptly came to a stop. We tried moving forward, and the bow came up, but we were again pulled down and stopped. We tried to move to the side, only to experience the same thing. We could move a little way, but if we tried to go farther, the bow would descend and we would stop.

We were able to determine what had happened. We had drawn one of the cables into a thruster duct and entangled it around the thruster propeller. One end of the cable was now firmly attached to **NR-1**, and the other end was shackled to the heavy metal structure,

Untangling the line was not possible. The thrusters were inaccessible outside the pressure hull. We were too deep for all but saturation divers, and there were none available. (A saturation dive, at that depth in the open sea, would have been <u>extremely</u> hazardous.) The Navy's submarine rescue system (the McCann Bell) could not mate with **NR-1**. (The Deep Submergence Rescue Vehicle (**DSRV**) – which became operational years later – would be similarly unable to link with **NR-1**.) Finally, the contact appeared to be firmly embedded in the bottom. A "brute force" lift – blowing all our ballast tanks – <u>*might*</u> pull it up with us, but that was an extreme, last resort measure.

With the reactor supplying light and heat, and with plenty of food and oxygen, we were not in any immediate danger. For the crew, this was just another **NR-1** challenge. (For Fred and Roger, it seemed <u>*far*</u> more serious.) We had a problem, to be sure, but we knew it was one we could solve. We just didn't know how.

We maneuvered until the fouled cable was visible in a viewport. It appeared to be stiff metal, about three inches in diameter, heavily encrusted with sea life. It was not clear why a metal cable extended *upward*.

The "jaws" of the SUBMARINE **NR-1** manipulator were two flat plates, and there were no sharp edges that could be used to cut the cable. We found, however, that if we gripped the cable in one spot, and twisted the manipulator jaws back and forth, we would eventually snap a strand of the cable. I was handed the manipulator control box, and I settled in for a long manipulator session – back and forth – back and forth …

It took more than two hours, but finally the cable parted. We were free. I stowed the manipulator, and we lifted off the bottom and cleared the area. The end of the cable, of course, was still tangled in the thruster propeller, but we were able to complete our mission using three thrusters. When we returned to port, the ship's divers removed the cable fragment from the thruster. A piece of the line was mounted on a plaque to commemorate the incident. The Sperry engineers decided that they liked designing and building submarines more than riding them. One never went to sea on **NR-1** again.

Surprisingly, the cable was not metal at all, but polypropylene line. The heavy accumulation of sea-growth had stiffened and disguised it. The cable was smaller than we had thought, only a little over one inch in diameter. Polypropylene floats, and this accounted for the cable's streaming upward.

After this incident, we modified the manipulator jaws to include cutting blades, like a good pair of pliers. We were learning as we went along, and that was one of the rewarding aspects of service on **NR-1**, but we really didn't need a crisis like this one to inspire us.

Royalty

This story is a little different from the others I have recorded. I had nothing to do with this event, and I only heard about it years later. At the time of the story, my Dad, Jason Maurer, was the admiral commanding the Naval Forces in Key West. As you will see, he played a central role. For years, we have had a framed photograph of the two principals that was taken in my parents' quarters at the Naval Station. This is the story behind that photograph.

It was April of 1972, and Dad had been Commander, Key West Forces, for a little less than a year. The bases in the area supported submarines and aircraft, and they were heavily involved in training. Key West was not on the "front lines" of the cold war, but it was not a forgotten backwater. On this day, April 14th, it would be thrust into a prominence that was as unusual as it was unexpected.

About mid-morning, the admiral observed a civilian helicopter landing on the concrete mole at the south-western edge of the submarine basin. No notice had come from the Key West Airport, three miles to the east, or from Boca Chica Naval Air Station, five more miles up Route 1. The aircraft could have experienced an in-flight emergency, or simply run short of fuel. In any event, something was amiss, and the Chief of Staff was dispatched to the helicopter to see what might be needed.

Shortly thereafter, the Chief of Staff returned, accompanied by the plane's crew and its passengers. Leading the party was His Majesty, Hussein, the King of Jordan.

The king was in civilian clothes, and it soon became clear that he neither expected nor desired any pomp or ceremony. His visit was completely unofficial and "off the record". Not only was it not a "state visit", no-one in Washington even knew the king was in the country. He was visiting friends on the east coast of Florida like any ordinary tourist, and he had flown down to Key West simply to see the area.

King Hussein briefly visited my parents' quarters and then he and my Dad walked over to the headquarters building. The king was introduced to the staff, and a splendid luncheon was assembled in his honor in the headquarters mess. Several of the staff wives were hastily sworn to secrecy and invited to join the party[5].

As lunch was drawing to a close, Dad asked the king if there was anything he wished to see or do during his visit. King Hussein thought for a moment (or at least appeared to!) and replied, "I really would like a ride on a submarine."

Dad asked the Chief of Staff which boat was the "ready submarine" that day, and he was told that the **USS SEA LEOPARD** was ready to get underway on a moment's notice. While the Chief of Staff called ahead, Dad walked the king and his party down to the **SEA LEOPARD**, where the boat's Commanding Officer, LCDR William Hayes, USN, was waiting to meet them at the brow.

---

[5] Mrs. Gladys McCarthy, Admiral Maurer's son's mother-in-law, recalls being told that this lunch was actually served in the Admiral's quarters, about a half-block away.

Dad asked LCDR Hayes to offer the king and his party a demonstration ride, including submerged operations, in the nearby submarine operating area. He added that he had complete confidence in the **SEA LEOPARD** and her crew, and he did not feel the need to accompany the king on the trip. King Hussein smiled his agreement and followed LCDR Hayes to the submarine's bridge, preparatory to getting underway.

When King Hussein was about to go down the hatch, he reached into his jacket, removed a rather large handgun and handed it to a young sailor saying "Would you please hold on to this for me?" Admiral Maurer reported that the look on the young man's face was priceless.

Dad walked back to the headquarters building, knowing that it was important to let official Washington know what was afoot. He called the Chief of Naval Operations, Admiral Elmo Zumwalt, USN.

"You can't do that", Admiral Zumwalt exclaimed. "We have to get permission! We have to notify the State Department! I have to call the President!"

The **SEA LEOPARD** was already underway.

"Relax, Bud", Dad said. "I know the Skipper. The king is in good hands. No-one needs to get excited over this. As long as the boat doesn't sink, and that isn't about to happen, this will all turn out just fine."

Several hours later, the **SEA LEOPARD** returned from sea. The boat had operated on the surface and submerged. King Hussein had taken a turn on the diving planes under the watchful eye of the qualified planesman. The king had toured the boat and shaken hands with every man in the crew. All in all, the trip had been enjoyed by every man on board, from king to seaman.

Dad met the ship and escorted King Hussein and his party to the helicopter. The helo lifted off, and Dad called Washington a second time to report that all was well.

There were no repercussions, and there was no publicity. Dad reiterated King Hussein's desire for "no publicity" to the staff, and the afternoon came to a quiet close.

Chips and Gates

An electronic technology that was widely used on the 1960s and 1970s was called "transistor-transistor-logic". TTL chips appeared in everything from consumer electronics to the most sophisticated military systems. The image of a small black plastic oblong, with a dozen or more metal connectors, has defined what many of us visualize today when we hear of a "chip".

My next door neighbor, George Scott, initially got me interested in TTL. In 1974, while I was on **BERGALL**, I pulled a muscle in my back, and I was down flat for several weeks. George brought me his old electronics hobby magazines to help pass the time. Years later, far at sea on **PARCHE**, his kindness paid off.

The family of TTL devices – essentially "building blocks" – could be connected in a variety of ways to accomplish almost anything a designer could imagine. One of the most basic chips was the "quad – 2 input AND gate". This chip had four separate "AND" gates (two inputs and an output) and two power supply connections, for a total of fourteen connections.

The four gates on this chip were completely independent. When an engineer was designing a circuit board, he could use one, two, three, or all four gates, as he desired. The choice of the gate or gates to be used was based simply on which connectors better suited the circuit board layout. The chip (even the premium military version) only cost about a dime, so there was not a lot of pressure to use all four gates. In many cases, only one gate was used, and the other three were simply not connected.

We had such a circuit in our ship's inertial navigation system, or SINS. The SINS was a critical piece of navigation equipment. It kept track of "where we were", and it provided important spatial and directional references[6]. One day, the SINS malfunctioned, and we traced it to a chip with the four AND gates. We had no way of knowing whether the entire chip or only the gate being used in that particular circuit was defective. As luck would have it, we had no spare.

I directed the electronic technicians to look elsewhere in the SINS for a similar circuit where a different gate was used, with a different group of three gates left unconnected. They found one. The two chips were exchanged, and the bad gate (so it turned out to be) ended up in an unused spot, unconnected. The SINS was back in commission, and we continued our mission.

---

[6] Notice that I say, "It kept track ..." Obviously, the SINS did more, but the equipment liked to be given a "starting point". This characteristic led many of us to say, "SINS is great. You tell it where it is, and it will tell you where you are."

Ice Cream

How to defuse a reprimand

BERGALL had one of the finest softball teams in the Atlantic Fleet.[7] We all loved the game, and it was natural for us to schedule a beer-ball game when we visited Roosevelt Roads for a brief stop-over. When **BERGALL** played softball, it was for real. Even the beer moved aside when someone stepped to the plate. After two games ("One is never enough …") in the hot Puerto Rican sun, however, we were dusty and tired.

The ship was moored nearby, and we tramped back. Swimming was not allowed off the pier, but we were the only ship in the Roads, and the cool water was *so* inviting….

First one, then two, then nearly the whole crew "accidentally fell" into the water. I was among them, and the water was wonderful.

Within about five minutes, the officer in charge of the harbor came running down the pier, spouting fire. "Swimming is not allowed! I want to see your Executive Officer, NOW!"

The crew pointed me out, and I sheepishly climbed out of the water. It was obvious that I would not do, and the officer demanded to see the captain. I dried off as best I could and then went below to get our Commanding Officer, CDR Ray Wyatt.

---

[7] We were runners-up in the Fleet-wide tournament, one year. Quite an accomplishment for a small ship.

"Captain, I'm afraid I've gotten you in trouble," I opened. "CDR H___ is topside. He's boiling mad because we were swimming off his pier."

Captain Wyatt rose, and in what I have ever since considered a stroke of absolute genius, he drew two large cones at our soft-serve ice cream machine. He carried them topside into the hot Puerto Rican sunshine and offered one to the commander who was waiting to read him the riot act.

Have you ever tried to chew someone out when you have to stop every few seconds to lick the ice cream that is threatening to melt all over your hand?

No Message to BERGALL

Unlike most of the stories in these pages, I was only peripherally involved in this incident. Indeed, I only learned of it weeks after it occurred. I have included it here because it says so much about the support we received from those who 'only watch and wait' when we went off to sea. I think you will agree that this is a story that deserves to be told.

A little background about communications to ships at sea is necessary. On a given day, a destroyer will receive dozens of naval messages. On a larger ship, particularly one with an embarked staff, the number will rise into the hundreds or more. A carefully constructed administrative and organizational system ensures that important messages are flagged for immediate attention, and that all messages are routed to the specific people that need to deal with a particular topic.

Messages may contain important changes to a ship's mission, time-sensitive weather predictions, intelligence estimates, or the latest status of important spare parts requisitions. On a surface ship, with its antennas always up in the air, reception goes on continuously, but the volume of incoming messages can still be a real annoyance. On a submarine, which has to slow and ascend toward the surface to receive a radio signal, this same traffic load could easily prevent the boat from executing its mission.

To solve this dilemma, all messages for a submarine at sea are routed through an organization that is familiar with the boat's mission and knows what it *really needs* on an immediate basis. This organization, often the submarine's parent squadron, then decides which messages should be broadcast to the ship and which can wait until the boat returns to port. The number of messages which must be transmitted is drastically reduced.

A brief word about the organization of a submarine squadron staff is also in order. One particularly important billet is that of the Squadron Secretary. This is a junior officer's billet that is often filled by a gentleman who has been commissioned from the enlisted ranks and who therefore has many valuable years of experience. This officer keeps the staff running smoothly, handling all the myriad administrative tasks and virtually all the paperwork. He is also the point of contact for any problems that may arise among the families of men on a deployed submarine.

Lieutenant (junior grade) Richard Gudis was Squadron TWO's Secretary. Dick was exceptional in his job. The Squadron ran smoothly, and Dick could handle any problem tossed at him. He was particularly adept at solving the knotty family crises that always seemed to surface when the man of the house was away. It was well known on the waterfront, however, that Dick had little sympathy for a "manufactured" crisis or a washing machine that should have been repaired long <u>*before*</u> its owner put to sea. Cry-babies were not tolerated. Dick was of the crusty breed that firmly believed that if the Navy had wanted you to have a wife, it would have issued you one. (Dick's *own* wife was a lovely lady, but you get the picture ...)

45

BERGALL was at sea, several weeks into a training mission that would last nearly three months. My wife discovered a medical problem that was more than a little scary: a lump in a breast. Surgery was called for.

The first part of the procedure would be a biopsy. If the growth was benign, the lump would be excised and Carol would be sent home. If the growth was cancerous, more radical removal would occur immediately. It was left to Carol to discuss these frightening possibilities with her husband.

Informing me, of course, would be difficult. I was far at sea. The hospital would have to send a message to BERGALL, advising me of what could happen. Carol did not want to disturb me with such a message, but the doctors were adamant: hospital regulations required that the spouse be informed.

Carol went to see Dick Gudis. She asked if there was *any* possibility that I could be dropped off in a friendly port, so that I could fly home and we could face the problem together. Dick did not know exactly where BERGALL was at that moment, so he excused himself to inspect the classified chart that depicted our expected track. When he returned, the news was not good. We had passed the "point of no return", and there was no possibility that I could get off the ship[8]. Carol would have to face the surgery – with its terrifying possibility – alone.

"All right", said Carol. "Here's what we will do. The hospital will send their message, informing Jack of what could happen. He can't

---

[8] This concept sounds heartless, but it was well understood and accepted by all of us – and by our families.

help – he can only worry, and that won't help anyone. I would like the Squadron to screen the hospital's message *off* the submarine broadcast. The hospital will never know, and Jack won't worry about something he can't control."

And that's what was done.

The lump was benign, and Carol recovered easily. But anytime thereafter, when Carol brought one of our boat's problems to Dick Gudis, his helpful response went far beyond even his own high standards.

Fourier Analysis

Fingerprinting individual radar sets

In any tactical situation, it is obviously helpful to know who the "players" are, or at least how many are in the game. After dark, when painted numbers are no longer visible, it gets harder. By intercepting electronic transmissions, like radar, it is possible to tentatively identify a given emitter by the characteristics of its signals.

BERGALL had an intercept receiver built in to one of her periscopes. Each sweep of a nearby radar would be heard as a buzz over the receiver. By counting the seconds between successive sweeps, we could determine how fast the radar was rotating. By routing the signal into an analyzer, we could determine another characteristic of the signal, called the pulse repetition rate, or PRR[9]. The PRR (about 500 cycles per second) determined this way was only accurate to the nearest integral cycle, but this number, combined with the rotation rate, was usually enough to identify the type of radar we were hearing.

Knowing the type of radar was helpful, but it did not identify a particular set, or the ship that carried it. We needed a better, more precise, identification.

---

[9] The analyzer used was a nothing more than an oscilloscope, paired with an audio tone generator. The radar signal went into one input of the oscilloscope, and the tone went into the other. When the frequency of the audio tone matched the radar PRR, the oscilloscope would flash a single loop (called a Lissajous figure) each time the radar swept by. By reading the tone frequency, you knew the radar PRR, but only to the nearest cycle per second.

Even when a radar antenna is not pointed at you, its transmission can be heard. The signal is obviously much weaker when the antenna is pointed away, but it *is* there. By turning up the gain on the intercept receiver, we could hear a faint, but constant, buzz. Each time the radar swept over us, of course, the buzz was LOUD!

Because the gain was turned up so far (the term is "the receiver was over-saturated"), the radar signal was severely distorted. But one thing you cannot distort is time. Even though the signal no longer exhibited the correct "shape", its frequency was not affected. By routing the signal into a Fourier analyzer normally used by the sonarmen, and allowing that analyzer to "churn" for several minutes, it was possible to determine the radar's PRR to several decimal places.

Using this technique, it is possible to tie a particular radar signal to the crystal, deep within a radar set's circuitry, that generates that set's pulse repetition rate. BERGALL could uniquely identify a ship by its radar, even when several ships had the same model.

Instead of determining that there were "several ships out there" with PRRs of "about 481 cycles per second", BERGALL could state with confidence that (for example) "there are four ships, with PRRs of 481.2567, 481.2532, 480.9842, and 481.1356 c/s, respectively".

Fourier analysis is arcane and somewhat esoteric mathematics. The equipment to perform this analysis is complex, and it was never intended to be used in his manner. This application came about because BERGALL personnel recognized an opportunity to use mathematics to meet a very real and immediate tactical need.

Roadhouse

When the commanding officer of a nuclear powered ship is due to be relieved, the incoming officer arrives several weeks before the formal change of command. This period affords the captain-to-be with the opportunity to become familiar with the ship, its material condition, and the state of training of its crew. It is a very trying time for both officers. The outgoing captain would like to present his ship in the best possible light, and the relieving officer is anxious to begin his new assignment.

It is a busy time. Inspections, demonstrations, audits, drills, underway operations. Capabilities are demonstrated, and readiness is assessed. Records are examined and personnel are interviewed. Every aspect of the ship is placed under a microscope and carefully reviewed. The days are full, but they pass slowly. The change of command period drags on, but the ceremony comes closer and closer.

My relief of **PARCHE'S** first commanding officer, CDR Richard Charles, USN, was a breeze. Dick had built a fine ship, and **PARCHE** was in fine mettle for the missions that lay ahead. The change of command would be in Charleston, and the ship would depart within a few days for our new assignment on the West Coast.

My family was planning to attend the change of command. Carol had come from the California, and my father and brother had come to Charleston from the Florida Keys. The afternoon before the ceremony, I arranged to take my family out to "the best steak dinner in town".

Being unfamiliar with Charleston, I asked the officers in the wardroom for their recommendations.

The officers were unanimous. The best steaks could be had in a small, out-of-the way restaurant outside the city. They provided driving directions and an admonition:

"Take Route (and they named the road) into the Carolina countryside, and just keep driving. When you're *sure* you've gone too far, keep going. It's a long way out, but it's worth the trip."

It was early evening when I piled Carol, my Dad and my brother into our rental car, and we started driving. We drove. And drove. We left Charleston civilization behind, and we drove some more. We were on a narrow, two-lane country road, and there was not another car in sight. Small farm-houses, each with a pick-up truck in the side yard, could be seen among the pines. And still we drove.

Finally, we were there. "Restaurant" is not the right term for what greeted us. "Roadhouse" is closer, but even it may be too grand. We were early, and the parking lot (unpaved, of course) was still empty. The building siding was faded and peeling - it was apparent that the building had seen better days. The windows were clean, with neon signs adorning every one. There was no litter.

My Dad was convinced. "The officers knew it was the last time they could put one over on the new captain. Let's face it, Jack, they got you."

Carol was adamant. There was no way she would set foot in "that place."

My brother, Peter, just chuckled.

But we had driven a long way. I really didn't want to admit defeat and return to town. I didn't believe the **PARCHE** officers would have been so discourteous (and perhaps, foolhardy) to send us on a wild goose chase. I told my family to remain in the car - I would take a look inside.

The room was brightly lit, and it spoke of linoleum and plastic. About ten square tables were spread around the eating area. Each table had four chairs, no two of which matched. A well-stocked bar extended the length of the room. The entire area was spotless.

And then I saw them. On the wall behind the bar were hung plaques from every submarine in the Atlantic Fleet and a few foreign navies.

I walked back to the car. "This is the place."

The steaks were probably the finest we have ever had.

Inside the Lock

Excitement in the Panama Canal

About a week after I assumed command of **PARCHE**, we steamed out of Charleston and turned south. We arrived a few days later at the Atlantic terminus of the Panama Canal, and our Canal Pilot came aboard.

Navy Regulations specifically list the only two times when a commanding officer is not responsible for the safe navigation of his ship. One occurs when transiting the Panama Canal under the control of a Canal Pilot.[10] This transfer of responsibility is very real. A Canal Pilot is not present to advise or recommend. For all intents and purposes, *it is his ship* and he really takes charge.

I turned the "conn" over to the Pilot, and we headed for the first lock. The Pilot ordered "standard" speed, about thirteen knots.

A submarine's appearance is deceptive. It displaces about five thousand tons, but most of this mass is hidden from view. At speed, this unseen mass makes for unrecognized momentum, which may be very significant, as we shall see.

As we entered the lock, still at thirteen knots, I turned to the Pilot. "Captain," I said. "I think you may want to slow down."

---

[10] The other occurs when a ship's bow crosses the sill entering a drydock. At that moment, the responsibility shifts to the shipyard's docking officer.

The Pilot asked, "You think I should slow?"

"No, I think you should STOP."

Still at thirteen knots, he asked, "You really think we need to stop?"

"No, I think you need to BACK FULL, NOW."

I finally had his attention, and he ordered the backing bell. The throttleman in the Maneuvering Room responded quickly to the emergency order[11], and the big propeller began to churn in the reverse direction. The power of a backing bell in a situation like this is impressive. Waves rebounded off the lock walls. Water covered the deck. We bounced around and finally came to a stop. The upper lock gate loomed over us, just a few yards away.

The gate gets closer every time I tell this story.

---

[11] Anytime you went directly from an "ahead" to a "back" bell, without ringing up "stop" first, the throttleman treated the new order as an emergency.

Swim Call

Recreation (?) in the Panama Canal

During our transit of the Panama Canal, enroute to **PARCHE'S** new home in the Pacific, we had to "step aside" for a ship proceeding in the opposite direction. We would have to wait in Gatun Lake for about three hours. I decided that we would move just outside the ship channel and drop the anchor. I checked with the Pilot, who reassured me that the water just outside the channel was adequately deep.

It was warm, and the fresh water of the Lake was inviting. I decided to hold "swim call", and we passed the word. Soon many of the crew were enjoying a refreshing swim next to the ship. True to submarine practice, we stationed a rifleman topside, but we recognized that a submariner with a loaded rifle was probably more dangerous than any shark ever hoped to be.

We arranged for short term watch reliefs, so that everyone could take advantage of the cool water. I asked the Canal Pilot if he would like to take a dip – I was sure we could rustle up some swimming trunks – but he declined.

After about two hours, the last crewman had left the water. We were getting ready to get underway again, and the Pilot joined me on the bridge.

"We still have time", I said. "Are you sure you don't want to take a swim?"

"No, thanks", he replied. "Too many alligators in that Lake."

Pumping the Dome

An object lesson in personal integrity

The spherical sonar array is mounted on an extension of the pressure hull at the forward end of a submarine. A thick Fiberglas fairing is attached to the bow and smoothes the flow of water past the array. (This fairing is the rounded surface that is visible on those dramatic emergency surfacing sequences you see on television.)

The space between the fairing and the array is normally filled with sea water, since the Fiberglas is not designed to withstand submergence pressure. When external maintenance on the array is required, the water in this space (incorrectly called the "sonar dome") is pumped out to permit access. This evolution, obviously possible only in port, takes several hours and results in the boat taking a dramatic "up angle" alongside the pier. It is, to say the least, uncomfortable and inconvenient. Refilling the dome when the maintenance is completed is an equally tedious evolution.

Before the dome is refilled, a careful inspection of the space is made, since any debris could rattle once the boat is underway. Being so close to the array transponders, any such rattle would effectively deafen the entire sonar suite.

One evening, a shipyard welder was working on PARCHE'S bow, near an open hatch to the sonar dome. While changing welding rods, the used rod slipped out of his hands and fell into the dome. The welder realized the consequences. We would have to pump the dome, make an entry and retrieve the dropped rod, and then refill the dome. We had many hours of work ahead of us.

The welder got up and informed the topside watch of what he had done. The watch called the duty officer, and because I was still aboard, the duty officer informed me. I told the duty officer that I wished to speak with the welder's supervisor, and the welder left to get him.

About a half hour passed, and the duty officer informed me that a very worried welder and his supervisor had returned. I went topside, and spoke to the supervisor.

"This man dropped a welding rod into the dome, and you both know what that entails", I said. "What you may not know, is that no-one else saw it happen. He could have quietly walked away, and no-one would have been the wiser. We would not have known we had a problem until our next underway.

"Instead, he immediately informed us of the slip. Now, we will be able to recover the rod before it causes a problem. His kind of personal integrity is rare, and it is much appreciated. This man can work on this ship anytime, and we will be honored to have him."

Tilt!

A lesson in perseverance

When the floor under your feet starts to lean, you know something is amiss. If you've had a few too many cold ones, you may not feel too chipper in the morning, but the problem will eventually go away. But when you're cold sober, and the floor in question is the deck of your submarine, and you're moored alongside the pier in your home port, you know something is seriously wrong.

PARCHE was slowly assuming a definite list to starboard. It had started slowly right after morning quarters, and by lunch time it was obvious to us all. We looked, but could find no ballast tank leaks. We checked tank levels. We ran the low pressure blower on all the ballast tanks until we were sure the tanks were dry. We reviewed all the maintenance in progress to be sure we were not causing the problem ourselves. We were not.

At our wit's end, we called the shipyard stability engineers for assistance. By then, it was mid-afternoon.

The engineers came down and took the same measurements we had taken. They recommended the same actions ("blow everything dry"), and to satisfy them, we complied. This time, the list started to come off. Within a couple of hours, we were back on an even keel, and I relaxed and went home.

The next day, it started all over again. This time, we called the shipyard right away, and the stability engineers came down while the list was still increasing. They took lots of readings and retreated to their reference books, drawings, and slide rules.[12] We still didn't know what was wrong, although the stability engineers had given us their best guess.

My Damage Control Assistant, Lieutenant Fred Schmorde, came up to my stateroom. He had a paper with some calculations that he had made.

"Captain," he said, "I don't know what the problem is, but it can't be what the shipyard says. Look here." He showed me his calculations, and I was convinced. He was right.

So, what *was* the problem? By this time, the list was going away again.

I suddenly realized what had been happening.

I took Fred up onto the quay. I picked up a length of pipe and tied one end of a ten-foot length of line to it. Dropping the pipe into the water, and holding on to the other end of the line, I started walking slowly toward the stern. When I came abreast of where the sternplanes were located, the pipe became snagged. The problem was solved.

When **PARCHE** moored at her accustomed berth at the quay on Mare Island, she was held clear of the wall structure by two large, inflatable fenders that held her off about five feet. During our last trip to sea, the shipyard had moved the after fender a few yards farther aft. It was now abreast of the portion of the ship that started tapering to a point. As a result, the stern planes were a couple of feet closer to the

---

[12] Remember slide rules?

wall. When the tide came in, the starboard sternplane stabilizer[13] would catch on a horizontal beam of the quay wall, and the starboard side of the ship could not rise with the tide. The boat would lean in the direction of the snagged stabilizer, exhibiting the starboard list. When the tide went out, everything would return to normal[14].

We slacked the lines, put the fender back where it used to be, and we had no more mystery lists.

We resolved this problem because something didn't seem right to Fred Schmorde, and he refused to let it go.

---

[13] Each sternplane had a vertical structure, called a stabilizer, at its outer edge.
[14] At that time of the year, Mare Island tides were not evenly diurnal. We had only one significantly high tide each day.

Five Links

A souvenir for the Captain

A reputation for "getting underway on time" is one that every ship aspires to, and **PARCHE** was no different. Our situation, however, was even a little more challenging than most: There is a shallow spot just south of the Richmond – San Rafael Bridge, and we were constrained to pass over it at high tide. If we missed our underway time by more than an hour or so, we would have to wait for the next tide. Even so, we did very well. I can only recall one time when we did not make it, and therein lies a story…

The anchor on **PARCHE** is normally held in place by two methods. First, the anchor chain is wound all the way "up" and the hydraulic mechanism is locked. Secondly, a set of jaws is moved inward and meshes with a collar on the anchor itself. These jaws positively clamp the anchor in place. Before we got underway, we would take a tension on the chain, retract the clamp, and "walk" the anchor out a few feet to make sure it was ready for use.

On the day in question, something was wrong. The clamp jaws appeared to retract, but the anchor would not come down. We tried to pull it up; we tried to ease it down. Nothing. This was going to take some time to repair. Reluctantly, I secured the Maneuvering Watch, shutdown the reactor, and we arranged for the shipyard divers to come and take a look.

I went back to the hydraulic mechanism and noticed that it tried to turn in the "down" direction, no matter which way we set the control. We disassembled the control valve and found the cause. A small link that positioned an internal spool had failed. As a result, the valve stayed in the "down" configuration, no matter how we tried to position it. When we had tried to lift the anchor so that we could retract the clamp, we were actually jamming the chain *down* into the hawse pipe.

Ever try to push a string? That's what we were doing, and the chain links were now solidly wedged in the hawse pipe.

We repaired the control valve, and the shipyard divers freed the anchor. They had to cut off a short length of anchor chain off in the process, and for several years, I had a six-foot-long souvenir. After several moves, however, Carol laid down the law: The heavy chain had to go. I saved five links, and the rest went away. I still have the five links.

Tight Fit

Alley Cat comes through

Mare Island Naval Shipyard was PARCHE'S home port. We got to know many of the shipyard workers quite well. They were a fine group of experienced professionals who took great pride in their contributions to the ship's success. Many of them felt that they only _loaned_ their boat to us. We were expected to take the boat to sea and bring it back undamaged.

One group of the workers was the Riggers. They were the men who drove the bobcats and delivered equipment to the ships. They transported pumps and pipes, motors and mechanisms, cables and condensers. Theirs was not a glamorous job, but vital nonetheless. And the best rigger in the yard was Alley Cat.

Alley Cat was a huge bear of a man. (I never knew his real name. but _everyone_ knew who Alley Cat was.) He had a full beard (unkempt) and long hair to match. His coveralls looked like they had been rolled around the bottom of a drydock just to make them comfortable. He _always_ looked disheveled, but no-one cared. He was _good_. And one day, I learned how good he was.

Now, I have to get technical. (Sorry!) Submarines have many pumps. Most of these take water from the ocean, push it through the tubes of a heat exchanger, and return it to the sea. They have sea pressure on both the suction and discharge of the pump. So, they don't care how deeply the submarine is submerged. They only need a couple dozen pounds of pressure. Two pumps, however, are different: The "trim" and the "drain" pumps have to be able to pump from inside the boat (zero pressure) to the ocean outside (submergence pressure). That is, they may have to generate _much_ more pressure than an ordinary circulating water pump.

They do this by combining several rotors on a single shaft. All the rotors turn together when the pump is run. Each rotor and its corresponding volute are called a "stage". The discharge of each stage is fed to the suction of the next stage, which then boosts the pressure and hands off the water to the next stage. With several stages, the necessary high pressure can be attained. Each of these two "multi-stage" pumps is about the size of a steamer trunk and weighs several hundred pounds.

Back to the story: our drain pump needed to be replaced. A replacement pump was located, flown to California, and delivered to the shipyard. All that was needed was to move the replacement to the Machinery Space and install it. And therein lay a problem.

We reviewed the pump plans and saw that the minimum projected dimension of the pump was twenty-one inches. (Imagine a light suspended far above the pump and projected downwards. The pump's shadow would be twenty-one inches across.) That was fine for the main hatch (25 inches in diameter) but too large for the two eighteen inch water-tight-doors that the pump had to pass through.

The pump _could_ be disassembled, and the smaller pieces passed through the doors. The pump would then be re-assembled at the installation site. However, we didn't want to do that. The pump had been assembled in a "clean" room, carefully balanced, and certified "quiet". That certification would be invalidated if we took the pump apart. Cutting a hole in the side of the submarine was an even more radical choice that was rejected immediately. What to do?

Now let's talk about the Riggers' favorite tool: a "chain-fall". A chain-fall is a heavy metal cylinder about the size of a basketball. It has three chains attached. First, a short, heavy chain permits hanging the device from a convenient pad-eye. The second is a longer, variable-length, heavy chain that is hooked to and supports the item to be lifted. The third chain is a lighter, continuous loop. Spinning this loop will adjust the length of the support chain. A single chain-fall weighs about thirty pounds, but several of them, properly used, will support an item weighing several hundred pounds.

Back to the pump. As a multi-stage pump, the sides were "fluted". That is, the pump sides edged in to "nestle" around each stage. Although the minimum *projected* dimension was twenty-one inches, the actual dimension at a given point could vary as the "flutes" edged in and out. A persistent rumor in the shipyard said that a trim/drain pump <u>could</u> pass through an eighteen-inch water-tight-door, but we couldn't see how. So that night I went to the one man who might be able to accomplish it.

"Alley Cat", I challenged. "I've got a case of premium beer for you and your crew if you can get that pump into the Machinery Space tonight."

I learned the next morning that a "chain-fall ballet" had wiggled the fluted pump through both water-tight-doors and into the Machinery Space. I was happy to buy the beer.

The 5000 Ton Calculus Trainer

Learning to hover

When I was at the Naval Academy, we were once told that we only needed to know three things to ensure a successful naval career:

- •Never belay a sheet.
- •F = mA
- •3, 5, and 8 are stackmen.

The first enjoined us to always be ready to slacken a sail if a puff of wind threatened to overturn a small sailboat. The last reminded us which men in a rifle squad had the crucial role in the order to "Stack Arms". F = mA is the fundamental law of force and acceleration, from which almost every law of physics can be derived. This last law became very familiar to the diving teams on **PARCHE**.

A submarine controls its depth in two ways. First, it has to be fairly close to neutral buoyancy. It has to "weigh" about as much as the water it displaces. Secondly, the diving planes, through the force exerted by the water flowing over them, compensate for minor discrepancies in buoyancy.

Buoyancy is controlled by flooding water into, or pumping water out of, internal tanks in the submarine. The water is distributed among several tanks to maintain proper fore-and-aft balance. A boat is said to be "in trim" when a correct combination of tank levels has been established.

The effect of the diving planes depends on the speed of water flowing over them. At low speeds, the planes have a small effect. At high speed, they can mask a drastic unbalance in the ship's buoyancy. A temporary loss of depth control at slow speed can be corrected by increasing speed. Conversely, a submarine on a high speed transit may slow several times a day to check its trim status.

When a submarine must hover, the effectiveness of the planes goes to zero, and the importance of being in trim becomes paramount. If the submarine is too heavy, it will eventually sink, and if it is too light, it will eventually surface. Achieving a "stop trim" is essential. The diving officer must pump or flood exactly the correct amount of water if the submarine is to stay on the ordered depth.

The only instrument available to the diving officer is the ship's depth gauge. By watching the gauge, he can determine if the ship is rising or descending, and he can develop a sense for "how fast" the depth is changing. But if the boat is rising, it is not necessarily light, and if it is sinking, it is not necessarily heavy. $F = mA$ relates the <u>F</u>orce on the submarine caused by the unbalanced buoyancy, the <u>m</u>ass of the submarine (about five thousand tons-mass), and the resultant <u>A</u>cceleration. The force and the acceleration are *vector* quantities, that is, they have an associated direction. The *direction* of the force and the *direction* of the acceleration are <u>always</u> the same (up or down). The direction of the velocity can be different.

It is important to note that it is the direction of the acceleration and not the direction of the velocity that determines the direction of the force. It is this direction that determines whether the boat is light or heavy. A boat can be rising (velocity up), but if it is rising more and more slowly, its acceleration is *down,* and it is heavy. The same rising boat, if it is rising faster and faster, has upward acceleration, and it is light.

All four combinations of velocity direction (up or down) and acceleration direction (up or down) can exist, but it is always the direction of the acceleration that determines if a boat is heavy or light. If the boat is heavy, the diving officer needs to pump. If it is light, he needs to flood.

A glance at the depth gauge is all the diving officer needs to determine if the boat is rising or descending, but to determine the acceleration, the diving officer needs another input: *time.* By measuring the time to change depth by one foot, and then repeating the measurement several times, the diving officer can determine the direction of the ship's acceleration, and this is the crucial clue he needs to decide whether to pump or flood.

These subjects seem complicated, but they are basic calculus topics. We needed to make them second nature to diving teams that spent very little time in calculus textbooks. We held a series of training sessions in the wardroom to familiarize the teams with the concepts. The difference between velocity and acceleration was explained in practical ship control terms that we could all relate to. The application of a seemingly obscure physics formula to a very familiar ship control evolution was soon understood and appreciated.

A stopwatch was found and stored on the diving stand. The diving officer could be seen reaching for it whenever the order came to "Hover". The diving teams soon became experts in this evolution, and PARCHE could achieve a perfect trim as fast as the ship could slow to a stop. Hovering became a routine evolution, and the diving parties became deservedly proud of their expertise. Their skill was to prove important in coming operations.

The diving teams did not realize it at the time, but their proficiency at achieving a perfect hover would stand them in good stead when the time came to go *backwards*, but that's another story.

Back 'er up!

Learning to go backwards

Each year, **PARCHE** would sail from Mare Island (near San Francisco) to San Diego. The industrial capabilities at Mare Island Naval Shipyard were indispensable to us, and that is why we were home-ported there, but the training installations at the Submarine Facility at Ballast Point were valuable also. It was important, for example, for the battle stations team to spend time in the Attack Trainer conducting simulated torpedo approaches. The transits along the California coast gave us time for ship-wide training. And liberty in San Diego wasn't half bad …

On one such trip, we were assigned an area off San Diego for night-steaming, and we planned to enter port the following morning. We could use the time as we saw fit. At the time, we were preparing for a complex mission which would commence in several months. Only a few senior officers in the wardroom knew what was in store. On this night, we would develop a new skill that might come in handy.

At supper, I picked up the sound-powered telephone and called the Officer of the Deck. I told him to order zero speed and go into a practice "hover". I knew that getting a perfect, slow-speed trim would be valuable later, and zero speed was as slow as we could go. As the ship slowed, we could hear the Diving Officer adjusting the water levels in the auxiliary ballast tanks as he sought a perfect balance. By

71

the time we finished dessert, the ship had stopped coasting, and we were in a perfect hover.

I walked up to the Control Room and told the Officer of the Deck to order, "Back, one-third." He acknowledged, and I turned as if to leave.

"Captain", he said. "If we stay with a backing bell, we'll probably gain sternway." He was noting that submarines were prohibited from backing down while submerged – it was considered too dangerous.

"Well, I certainly hope so", I replied. And then I provided additional instructions.

"Limit your astern speed to five knots. Tell the planesmen to experiment to find the best combination of stern plane and sail plane control actions. When you're satisfied with their ability to maintain depth, try some depth changes. First fifty feet, then a hundred, then more – up and down. Again, let the planesmen experiment – they're the experts. Limit the ship's angle to ten degrees. If you get into trouble, order 'Ahead, standard'[15] until you are going forward and regain control."

I gave the OOD some depth limits and then left the Control Room.

An hour or so later, the OOD called. "Captain, we're backing just fine, but we're about to leave our assigned area."

"Well", I answered. "Put the rudder over and back around. Turn as necessary to stay two miles inside the area boundary."

---

[15] Any order which changed direction, without pausing at "Stop", would be treated as an emergency. The Throttleman would answer the bell promptly, without regard for the cavitation noise that would ensue.

For the rest of the night, we backed around our area off San Diego. The diving teams of each watch sections learned – with themselves as the best teachers – to back down, submerged, safely. We learned how to maintain depth and how to change it. We learned how to control the angle on the ship. We developed "thumb rules" that told us when to level off during an ascent or descent.

When a watch section was relieved, each planesman proudly passed his new skills on to his relief. Each man voluntarily "stuck around" until the on-coming section was comfortable with the new techniques.

The word spread through the crew and quite a few of them gathered at the aft end of the Control Room to observe the unusual evolutions. At the time, few people knew why this skill might later become important. Most of them just considered that it was just "another one of the Captain's weird ideas". Later, the value of being able to confidently maneuver the ship in unusual situations would become apparent. Although we never had an operational requirement to back down, it was a skill we knew we had, and we knew we could call on it if needed.

We learned an unexpected, but valuable lesson along the way: The ship's inertial navigation systems (SINS) used ship's speed, as reported by the electromagnetic log, as a "damping" signal for increased stability. For electronic reasons, the log treated all motion as "forward" – it was never designed to operate in reverse. We learned that it was better to switch the SINS to an "un-damped" mode when we practiced backing down. The SINS did not like having to operate without its stability input, but at least it was not fed erroneous information. Far better to learn this precaution during a training session than on a mission ...

The pride and confidence developed in the planesmen – among the most junior (and vocal!) men on board – when their judgment and skills were trusted to develop the new techniques were infectious. The entire crew learned that "their opinions counted." It was a lesson that stood us in good stead over and over again. Several of the stories in these pages are built around an idea or contribution from one of these fine men.

Configuration Control

Unauthorized modification

Submarines are complex beasts. Literally hundreds of systems and thousands of components combine to make a truly magnificent machine. A ship like PARCHE can go to far places, accomplish marvelous feats, and return safely. Many programs (and many people) contribute to this success.

It starts with the designers. Thorough analysis in meticulous detail goes into every component. Every aspect of the design is carefully explored. Next are the builders. The skills and experience of shipyard people go into every component. When all is done, the finished product is handed to the crew to operate.

The role of the engineers and administrators at the Naval Sea Systems Command (NavSea) in Washington does not stop when the ship goes to sea. Detailed records permit NavSea to know exactly what version of every component is installed on each ship. They know what improvements (ShipAlts) should be sent to a ship and when those modifications have been installed. They know when new spare parts may be needed, and they send them. It takes more than ships and crews to make a Navy.

The crew operates, but it does not design, build or modify. We were emphatically _not_ authorized to alter the ship.[16]

---

[16] One submarine Commanding Officer was relieved of his command when he lowered the pressure in his hydraulic systems to reduce oil leaks. His action

Sometimes, particularly with a handpicked crew like **PARCHE'S**, that policy was hard to accept:

Electronics Technician Second Class Woodson was *sharp*. He had been to many advanced classes, and he always graduated at or near the top of his class. One day, he approached and asked to show me something.

(A little technical background information is in order: Our Ship's Inertial Navigation System (or SINS) was a vital piece of equipment. It is also used on aircraft carriers (it's helpful to tell returning planes where the carrier is). The SINS has a data connection which can be connected to a printer, and this data can be useful for diagnosis of a SINS problem. On submarines (which have less room than aircraft carriers - !), the printer is not installed.)

Petty Officer Woodson led me to the SINS. He had designed and built an interface board which permitted him to connect the SINS to another piece of equipment that had a printer built in. He had bought the components (with his own money) at a local Radio Shack. The interface worked like a charm.

"Woody", I exclaimed. "We can't do that. This is a fine idea, but you have cross-connected two vital pieces of navigation equipment, and we deploy in three days. Take the board out, and while we're

---

inadvertently invalidated the ship's flooding recovery studies, which relied on high pressure hydraulic power to shut hull valves quickly.

deployed, write up the design and we'll submit it to the design bureau."

The board was removed, and this improvement was submitted. Petty Officer Woodson was formally commended for his skill and initiative. How could you not succeed with people like this?

Crossing the Bar

A tragic lesson in seamanship

About a mile and a half outside the Golden Gate, the San Francisco Bar rises to about ten fathoms (sixty feet) below the surface. This depth leaves plenty of water for even the large supertankers that enter the Bay, but the bar can have an unusual effect on a ship passing over it. This interaction was responsible for the tragic death of a submarine commanding officer a few years before **PARCHE** came to the Bay Area.[17]

I do not understand the exact mechanism of the interaction, but its effect is very real and very frightening. When a submarine crosses the bar, particularly in the outbound direction, a resonance is somehow established between the ship and the waves rolling in from the Pacific. Many times, the wave action is not obvious on the surface, and the seas appear deceptively calm. The effect manifests itself in large, slow, but inexorable vertical motions of the ship.

The submarine rises, pauses, and then slowly sinks until the sea surface is just below the top of the sail. On a submarine with a small, low sail, water can pour down the bridge hatch or gently lift bridge personnel over the side and into the sea.

The immediate reaction when this starts to happen is to slow down, but this only makes the vertical motion worse. The first time we

---

[17] Cdr Alvin L. Wilderman, USN, Commanding Officer of the **USS PLUNGER**, was lost over the side while crossing the San Francisco bar on November 30, 1973. Sailor, rest your oar.

observed this phenomenon on **PARCHE**, we ended up creeping over the bar at three knots, hoping that the rising water would not come any higher. (The hatch was shut, and bridge personnel were in safety harnesses, but it was still frightening.)

We learned that the best way to counter the effect was to put the stern planes on "rise', and to charge ahead at a full bell (on the surface, about seventeen knots). We took lots of spray over the bridge, but it was only spray – not solid water. It was wet, and it was cold, but it was safe.

The phenomenon and our precautionary procedure were written up and submitted to the ComSubPac, where they were included in the standing Operation Order for Pacific Fleet submarines. We had lost one CO, but we would lose no more.

Epilogue

In October of 2004, the **USS PARCHE** was decommissioned. At a dinner before the ceremony, an after-dinner speaker recalled my pointing out this procedure to him twenty years earlier. At that time, the speaker was a lieutenant on one of the submarines in San Diego, and I had left **PARCHE** and joined the Squadron Three staff. The lieutenant's boat was going to the shipyard for overhaul, and it would soon have to pass over the San Francisco bar. The procedure I have described in this story was required, but the requirement was not well known, and my "reminder" was timely.

The speaker who still remembered my advice was Rear Admiral Paul L. Sullivan, USN, the Commander of the Pacific Fleet Submarine Force.

Darn. A sunny day ...

Navigation training on San Francisco Bay

The San Francisco Bay area is renowned for its fog. For years, poets and songwriters have extolled the quiet beauty and peacefulness of a mist-shrouded city. And I must admit, it was extraordinary to hear the traffic directly above us on the Golden Gate Bridge, and be totally unable to see any part of the bridge itself. But on some days, the "City by the Sea" was simply breathtaking. The sun would be out and the skyscrapers and the hills would be bright. The air would be clear and you could see forever.

These were the days that Pat McGahan hated the worst.

Lieutenant Commander Patrick McGahan was **PARCHE'S** navigator, and as fine a navigator as any commanding officer could hope for. During his tour, he would confidently guide **PARCHE** to far and distant places, in all kinds of weather. But he hated sunny days on San Francisco Bay.

Normally, a submarine navigator plots his positions using visual bearings on objects seen through a periscope. A prominent object is sighted, and its bearing is plotted on the chart. Several of these, taken nearly simultaneously, will result in a tiny triangle where the bearing lines cross, and this represents your position. Knowing where he is, the navigator can then recommend what course to steer to avoid hazards.

A well-trained navigation team can repeat this cycle (take a fix – plot it – recommend a course) once a minute.

When fog closes in, radar ranges are substituted for visual bearings. This process is *much* more difficult. Radar ranges are not as precise, and radar images may be hard to interpret. Lines on the chart may not correspond exactly to what the radar "sees". ("Is that image the edge of the beach, or the cliff behind it?") The demands on every member of the navigation team are greater, and the need for constant training is greater.

And that is why Pat hated clear weather. When **PARCHE** entered San Francisco on a clear day, anyone could navigate safely just by looking around. There was plenty of room. If you were not about to hit Alcatraz Island, and you weren't about to hit a pier in the city, then you were in good water. You could see where you were headed just by looking out over the bow. For the most part, you didn't *need* the Navigator or his team.

On such days, I would order the periscopes lowered and the radar raised. The navigation team would shift to their "reduced visibility" mode and they would begin navigating based on radar ranges. The pressure on the navigation team was acute, because I would tell the Officer of the Deck beside me on the bridge to use the navigator's recommended courses as long as we were not standing into obvious danger. As far as the Navigator was concerned, this was "the real thing."

There was a significant difference that made the navigation team's task <u>much</u> more difficult. Normally, when you encounter reduced visibility conditions, you slow down. On these days, since visibility on the bridge was unlimited, we would stay at standard speed – about thirteen knots. The distance between the Navigator's fixes would be three or four times as great as they would be in real reduced visibility conditions. Because the OOD was *following* the Navigator's recommendations, those recommendations were still expected to be good.

There was another important difference. The navigator of a Navy ship has a legal responsibility to navigate safely. In this situation, I was requiring Pat to operate with reduced capabilities, *without slowing the ship*. (Slowing down would have been his first recommendation in a real fog.) Accordingly, I directed the quartermaster to make an official entry in the Ship's Log to the effect that "the Commanding Officer has directed the Navigator to function with reduced capabilities for training, and the Commanding Officer has accepted all Navigation responsibilities on the bridge." Fortunately, I never had occasion to regret this entry!

The training was invaluable. The Navigator learned which landmarks provided effective triangulation, reliable ranges and good positions. The radar operator learned which fuzzy image was the real return for a given landmark. The sonar supervisor (who had his own chart in the sonar room) knew which buoys had chain rattles that he could hear and when the bearing to those rattles could be factored effectively into the Navigator's routine. The entire navigation team developed a rhythm for reduced visibility data recording, plotting, and projecting. All of these contributed directly to the Navigator's ability to provide useful recommendations to the Officer of the Deck.

The team got so good, that when we finally encountered a real fog, and we did slow down, navigation was a piece of cake.

One of Ours

Recognition training

PARCHE was assigned to Submarine Development Group One in San Diego, and the DevGroup was a component of Submarine Group Five, also at Ballast Point. Periodically, a senior officer from one of those organizations would ride us to observe our performance. On one occasion, our guest was the Chief of Staff of the Submarine Group, Captain Ned Kellogg.[18]

Captain Kellogg had learned that a contingent of destroyers would be transiting north along the California coast at about the same time we were scheduled to come out through the Golden Gate. The destroyers were proceeding to the Rose Festival in Oregon, and we would be conducting routine training off San Francisco. Captain Kellogg arranged for us to intercept the transiting destroyers, and to monitor their actions as if they were an enemy. The destroyers, in turn, would try to discover our presence. It promised to be good training for all concerned, and it would require no additional funding or ship time.

I recall that the day was bright and clear. A stiff wind was blowing, at least force six,[19] and the seas were rough. Maintaining our depth, near the surface, was difficult. When the destroyers were sighted to the south, it was obvious that they were feeling the seas even more than we were. They were traveling as fast as the conditions would

---

[18] Capt Kellogg, a fine gentleman and an outstanding submariner, had been the Executive Officer of my first ship, the USS SCAMP.

[19] About twenty-five knots.

allow, but the ocean was handling them roughly. The ships' bows would rise up on each wave, exposing their sonar domes, and then plunge downward into the next wave. It was apparent that they would be unable to hear us, and the rough seas made a visual sighting of our periscope unlikely.

We drove ahead to get a closer look, while our "adversaries" forged onward toward Portland. The destroyers sped past and disappeared to the north, while we prepared to commence our own training. Captain Kellogg asked my Officer of the Deck to describe what he had seen. What class of ship? How many guns? What mast configurations?

The OOD stumbled, and Captain Kellogg turned to me, since I had also been on the periscope. I couldn't do any better.

"Captain", I said. "If that had been a Kashin, a Krivak, or a Sovremenny[20], my officers could have told you the class, the radar configuration, the sonar capabilities, the name of the watch officer, and what he had for breakfast. In our recognition training, we do not expend effort on friendly combatants. All we need to know is that these ships were painted gray and flew the Stars and Stripes."

Captain Kellogg smiled his agreement.

---

[20] Three classes of Soviet destroyers.

Surfacing

A simple evolution – done well

There is no "punch line" in this story. There is no humor, no conflict, no problem to be solved. It describes an ordinary evolution that is repeated hundreds of times a day, by submarines of all nationalities. Yet this incident has remained in my memory for decades. I share it with you now, only because is special to me.

When a submarine puts to sea for a short time, she will often carry representatives of the boat's parent squadron or group. These men are tasked with observing the boat's performance, and the visits afford the senior officers in that boat's chain of command the opportunity to determine how well a boat is run. On this simple transit from Mare Island to the submarine base in Bangor, we had such a rider. Captain Ned Kellogg was a highly experienced submariner and a most pleasant shipmate. He was the Chief of Staff at Submarine Group TWO, and he was our "guest" for this trip – a trip that was nearing its completion.

It was a clear, cold winter night. We had left the Pacific about nine the previous evening, and we were proceeding eastward, toward Seattle, in the Strait of Juan de Fuca. The Strait was wide and deep, and we were submerged, making moderate speed. All was quiet and comfortable. We planned to surface at the eastern end of the Strait, and then proceed south-eastward into the Hood Canal and our berth at the Submarine Base.

About two in the morning, we were northeast of Port Angeles, and it was time to surface. Surfacing was a frequent evolution on older, diesel boats, but the advent of nuclear power meant that boats would often submerge and surface only once per trip. Additionally, the modern surfacing evolution was a little more complex than the older procedure. Because the evolution was both complex and infrequent, a boat's commanding officer would often supervise. The evolution also provided an excellent opportunity for a rider to gauge a boat's performance. Both I and Captain Kellogg were up.

Captain Kellogg was in the forward, starboard corner of the Control Room, where he could see and hear everything that went on, without being in any watch stander's way. I was a little farther removed, sitting on a bench locker in the aft, starboard corner of the Room[21]. The Officer of the Deck was Lieutenant David Antanitis. My written Night Orders told the Watch to be ready to surface at 0200.

A word about noise in the Control Room is in order. Every submarine preaches a quiet room, but on **PARCHE** we were fanatical about it. If you were in the Control Room, whether on watch or not, you *did not speak* except in the performance of your duties. There were *no* quiet conversations about the last port or the liberty to come. Orders were given in a soft, conversational tone. The OOD *never* had to raise his voice to make himself heard.

---

[21]   I remained in this location throughout the evolution.

Shortly before two in the morning, Lt. Antanitis ordered the Control Room "rigged for black" to allow his eyes to get used to the dark before he had to peer through the periscope. Dim glows from gauges and indicators provided just enough light for watch standers to quietly execute their tasks. The OOD slowed the ship, came a little shallower and turned slightly to one side. (This allowed the sonarmen to search the area behind us, where they were normally deaf.)

When he was satisfied that there was no-one behind us, Lt. Antanitis returned to base course, walked back to my corner and made his report.[22]

> "Captain, we're on course zero nine five, ahead one third, at one hundred fifty feet. I have cleared baffles and hold no contacts. Request permission to come to periscope depth."

> "Proceed to periscope depth," I responded.

Lt. Antanitis acknowledged the order ("Proceed to periscope depth, aye") and ordered the Diving Officer of the Watch to proceed smartly to five nine feet. Like most good OODs, Mr. Antanitis increased speed for a short time to help the DOOW ascend to a new depth. Then, he proceeded to the periscope stand and prepared to raise the periscope.

As soon as the scope head broke the surface, Lt. Antanitis spun the periscope and reported, "No close contacts." He ordered the Chief of

---

[22] By procedure, the Officer of the Deck was required to report certain steps to the Captain and obtain his permission to move to the next step.

the Watch to "prepare to surface without air"[23]. The word was passed over an announcing circuit, and throughout the ship, watch standers opened and closed valves, realigned dampers, and adjusted equipment settings in readiness for surfacing.

There was no conversation. No-one called out, "Where's the wrench? Where's the connector?" The drain valve to the bridge access trunk was opened (no water appeared) and the lower hatch was opened. The submarine identification beacon[24] and the bridge "suitcase"[25] were brought to Control. Prospective lookouts broke out foul weather jackets. When the preparations for surfacing were complete, Lt. Antanitis again walked back to my corner of Control and made his report.

> "Captain, we're on course zero nine zero, ahead one third, at five nine feet. I hold no contacts. The ship is prepared to surface without air. Request permission to surface the ship."

> "Surface the ship."

> "Surface the ship, aye."

---

[23] The "without air" aspect is a bit of a misnomer. Nuclear submarines, with essentially unlimited power, could drive themselves up to where the low pressure lower could "reach" the air and blow into the ballast tanks. The stored high pressure in the air banks was not used. This saved wear and tear on the air compressors, and this was our normal surfacing technique.

[24] The submarine identification beacon is a rotating amber light on a short pole that slipped into a small hole on the top of the bridge. The distinctive light served to warn other vessels that this small black shape was in fact a five thousand ton ship.

[25] The "suitcase" contained communication and alarm links that, when plugged in, effectively connected the OOD on the bridge with the watch standers in Control.

Lt. Antanitis gave the orders, and the Control Room watch standers quietly went into action. Speed was increased, and the diving planes went to full rise. When the boat was holding at a keel depth of around forty-five feet, the low pressure blower was started and air began to enter the ballast tanks. Lt. Antanitis prepared to shift his watch to the bridge.

When an individual went up the bridge access trunk to prepare the bridge area for surface operations, he would be out of communications with the watch standers in Control. If he were the Officer of the Deck during that period, no-one would be in charge of the ship. Not a good thing.

The answer was simple. Another qualified officer was called to Control, and the duties and responsibility of the Officer of the Deck were formally transferred to him. Once *completely* divested of the Watch, Lt. Antanitis was free to don his own foul weather suit, and to prepare to climb to the bridge.

Lt Antanitis and the lookout climbed up the access trunk and rigged the bridge for surface operations. The clamshells[26] were opened, equipment was installed and connected, and communications to Control were tested. When he was fully ready to re-assume his duties and responsibilities, Lt. Antanitis called the Officer of the Deck in Control, and a second formal relief ensued.

When he was once again the Officer of the Deck, Lt. Antanitis ordered "ahead, standard", and set course for Bangor.

---

[26] The "clamshells" were two hinged plates that faired the top of the sail for submerged operations. When the bridge was rigged for surface, they were swung out of the way.

Captain Kellogg and I left Control. Captain Kellogg had never said a word. As he passed, he said to me, "Now, I have seen excellence in action."

Mission Philosophy

Test, test, test 'em again

Since many of the stories in these pages involve imaginative repairs, it would be easy to conclude that submarines, and PARCHE in particular, are "buckets of bolts", just waiting for some component to fail. I assure you, that is not the case. It was emphatically not the case on PARCHE. For every part that failed, there were literally thousands that performed perfectly, often under conditions that far exceeded their designers' expectations.

This was not accidental. The engineers and procurement administrators at the Naval Sea Systems Command did a truly magnificent job. Our equipment and components were carefully designed, rigorously tested and scrupulously maintained. Reliability and redundancy were built in. We received the best, and we kept it that way.

The PM (preventive maintenance) program on PARCHE was extensive and all-inclusive - it covered everything. The program was formal and sacred – a scheduled PM got first priority. Nothing was left to chance. Every component – every piece of equipment – was repeatedly tested. Some of the tests were straightforward ("Did the light come on?") – some were more complex ("Is that bearing emitting supersonic tones that warn of degradation?").

Most of the tests were probably unnecessary, but we couldn't know which one, so we did them all. And then we did them again.

The "test everything" philosophy extended to mission operations. We never did anything on a mission that had not been tried and proven earlier, under realistic conditions. There is a "first time" for everything, but our first times were always _before_ we deployed. Every evolution, no matter how trivial, was conducted during our training days off San Francisco and San Diego.

This "try it all" philosophy was embraced by every member of the crew – officer and enlisted. The formal "Find every single point failure" program that identified the carbon dioxide check valve problem (described elsewhere in these pages) is a good example. The submerged backing skill (also described) is another.

In spite of our efforts, however, we were sometimes confronted by unusual circumstances and failures we had never considered. But those make good stories …

Graphical Integration

Once, it became necessary to determine <u>exactly</u> how far **PARCHE** had moved during a certain time period. We had an instrument that printed our north-south and east-west speeds every few moments, but we had no indication of distance travelled, and *that* was the information we needed.

Our speed as we moved was a function of ocean currents, the ship's mass, the propeller speed, and a host of other parameters. Many of those parameters changed, in some way, over time. Clearly, this was a very complex function, and it was obvious that an analytical solution was not possible. What to do? We <u>had</u> to find the distances, somehow.

We recalled from our college calculus that speed was the first derivative of position (or, spoken differently, that position was the integral of speed), but since we could not come up with a clean function for our speed, calculus could take us no further.

Or could it? Perhaps we could use the basic concepts of calculus to our advantage.

We covered the wardroom table with quartermasters' graph paper. We selected appropriate scales, and plotted our "speed vs time" points. A line was faired through the points, and then we literally counted the squares on the graph paper that lay beneath the line. In short, we determined "the area under the curve". Basic calculus. We applied appropriate scale conversions, and the result was a distance.

We did this twice, once for north-south motion and once for east-west, and we had our final position.

Subsequent events proved our calculations were perfect.

Timing is everything ...

A problem in Radio that really had me worried

Time was running out. We were well past our normal broadcast reception interval, and if we did not receive a message soon, we would have to abort our mission and head for home. It was not a comforting option.

Our radio receivers steadfastly refused to decrypt the incoming messages. All we received was a garble of meaningless characters. On this mission, **PARCHE** was not allowed to transmit, so we had no way to tell people that we had a problem. Our operation order was crystal clear on the subject: if we found ourselves unable to copy our broadcast for a specified length of time, we were to abort.

We tried alternate frequencies; we tried alternate broadcasts. We double-checked, then triple-checked, our crypto settings. We had different people set the equipment up. We ran every possible diagnostic test on our equipment, and the equipment passed every test. We even installed a backup radio, and then ran all the diagnostics on the backup. It, too, passed every test, but still we received only garbles.

By then I was "living" in a corner of the radio room. I was trying to stay clear of the working radiomen, but I was concerned. Very concerned.

The corner of the room where I sat was normally occupied by the ship's electronic technicians. The equipment there was designed to receive and analyze incoming radar signals. We were not using this capability now, and this was a good spot to stay out of people's way.

A nearby equipment panel included a small digital clock display, which the technicians used to make precise entries in their logs. I noticed that this clock was about a second and a half different when compared to the super-accurate atomic clock farther down the radio room.

At least one of the clocks was wrong.[27]

The atomic clock was a precision electronic instrument that was taken to a submarine tender or shipyard facility for calibration about a week before a deployment. In use, the clock's output was electronically supplied to the radio receiver, where the exact time was fed to the cryptanalytic circuits. If the atomic clock was wrong, the radio would simply not know what time it was. Without an accurate time signal, the equipment could not decrypt the incoming broadcast.

It was easy enough to learn which clock was wrong. We tuned in WWV (like every Boy Scout with a short wave radio) and we soon established that the atomic clock was the errant one. Somehow, we had to reset it, and the tender calibration equipment was many miles away. Worse, the radio technical manual stated that the incoming time signal had to be accurate to within a very small fraction of a second for the crypto equipment to "lock on."

The atomic clock had a "slew" switch that functioned like the tiny knob on a wrist watch to advance or retard the indicated time. This is what the tender personnel used to set the instrument correctly. Our problem was that we had no way of knowing how far to slew the clock

---

[27] A man with two watches never knows what time it is.

to match it with the actual time. And as I said, we had to get darned close.

I walked into the Sonar Room. "Do you guys still have that dual-trace oscilloscope?"

They did, and we carried it into Radio. We connected one set of leads to a radio room speaker, and fed that speaker from a radio tuned to WWV. The other end of the leads was connected to the upper trace on the oscilloscope. The audible "time tick" on WWV produced a visual spike in the oscilloscope display.

A second set of leads connected the output of the atomic clock to the lower trace on the oscilloscope. We could now slew the atomic clock back and forth until its "tick" was directly under the spike that came from WWV. This effectively set the atomic clock to the correct time. We disconnected all the test equipment and hooked the atomic clock back up to the radio.

We all held our breath as the crypto circuits synchronized themselves with the incoming broadcast. Within a few seconds, the synchronization was complete, and the radio printer presented us with absolutely beautiful, *readable* text.

Carbon Dioxide

A Parche Crewman comes through with flying colors

Several months before we departed on an important mission, I presented a task to the **PARCHE** wardroom, with the intent that they in turn pass the requirements to the Chief Petty Officers, the Leading Petty Officer of each division, and on to the entire crew. I wanted people to identify every single-point-failure location or situation on the ship. A single-point-failure was defined as a component or capability for which we had no installed duplicate, and no spare.

We would then take the necessary action, while we still had time, to secure some form of redundancy.

The task was not as daunting as it sounds. We had many systems and components where a "port" unit was matched by an equivalent "starboard" unit. All of these could be eliminated immediately. Many pieces of electronics were backed up by a complete spare unit, or their functions could be assumed by other equipment. These also could be dropped from consideration. As the weeks wore on, very few actual single-point-failures came to light. The submarine's designers had done well.

One day, a junior petty officer from the Auxiliary Division asked me to come back to the engineering spaces with him.

"Captain, I know we have two CO_2 scrubbers, but I've traced out the pipes, and the discharge lines from both of them join and go through that little check valve up there. If that check valve fails, we have a single-point-failure. We can't get carbon dioxide off the ship."

99

We both knew that the check valve was not likely to fail *shut*, but this was exactly the kind of engineering diligence that I wanted to encourage.

"Well, Johnson", I asked. "What do you propose?"

Petty Officer Johnson had worked out an answer. "With the right adapter", he said, "we can remove the discharge pressure gauge from one of the scrubbers, attach a sea chest blow hose[28], and discharge out through a nearby sea chest."

"Can you get an adapter?" I asked.

"Captain, I've got friends in Shop 38. I can take care of it,"

My response was easy. "Make it so."

Fast forward to the mission. We were under the ice, and one CO_2 scrubber was in operation, cleaning our air and pumping the carbon dioxide overboard. I received a call from the Officer of the Deck.

"Captain, #2 scrubber is lifting its relief. The Engineer has been notified.""

The Engineer joined me at the scrubber, and sure enough, the relief valve was lifting and dumping the carbon dioxide back into the boat. It was just as if Petty Officer Johnson's check valve had jammed shut.

"Call Johnson," I told the Engineer.

---

[28] Sea chest blow hoses were rated for submergence pressure. They could be hooked up if a sea chest for a piping system got clogged with seaweed or debris. One shot of air was always enough to clear out the sea chest and restore normal water flow.

Ten minutes later, Johnson came back to the engineering spaces, still rubbing the sleep from his eyes. We explained the problem to him.

"Do you think you can help the Engineer a bit?" I asked.

A grin spread across his face. "I think I can, Captain."

"Fine", I said. "Show the Engineer what you have, and then do whatever he tells you. I'm going back to bed."

Johnson's adapter worked perfectly. The check valve had not jammed shut, but an ice block had formed in the single overboard penetration, and the effect on system operation was the same. While we operated with Johnson's sea chest hose scheme, the ice in the line melted, and we were able to adjust the chemicals in the scrubber discharge, lowering its freezing point. Five hours later, we returned to normal operation and had no further problems.

Petty Officer Johnson received an official commendation for his contribution.

Too Much Air

An unusual problem, more hazardous than it appears

This story is a little technical. You will probably encounter more information about air that you ever wanted to know. But the story is unusual, maybe even unique, and the predicament into which we found ourselves was actually quite dangerous. At the time, we did not realize that we had a problem. Read on:

We all know that the air we breathe is about 20% oxygen. We live under about fifteen pounds per square inch of pressure[29], though we don't feel the weight of the atmosphere pressing on us. In a different measurement system, this pressure is about 760 millimeters of mercury.[30] Thus, oxygen accounts for about one fifth of the air pressure that bears down on us.

This "partial pressure" of oxygen (actually about 140 mm-Hg) is what our bodies need. Our bodies don't care about the *percentage* of oxygen, they want 140 mm-Hg.[31]

When submarines are deep, they often bleed oxygen from storage bottles into the ship to make up for the oxygen that is slowly depleted by people breathing (which *is* permitted, by the way). The bleed

---

[29] In fact, 14.6 psi (pounds per square inch) is often referred to as "one atmosphere" of pressure.
[30] "Millimeters of mercury" (mm-Hg) derives from the distance pressure will push a column of mercury up in a barometer. The measurement system is used mostly by meteorologists. For our purposes, 14.6 psi = 760 mm-Hg.
[31] Thus, mountain climbers and aviators need a richer (higher oxygen percentage) mixture when they ascend into thinner air.

system automatically keeps the partial pressure of oxygen at a safe level of about 140 mm-Hg. OK, got everything? Now here's the story:

One evening, I was lying in my bunk, and something didn't sound right. I couldn't put my finger on it, but something was wrong. I called the Officer of the Deck and asked him to check the ventilation system. It sounded like a damper might be mis-positioned, or a fan might be running at the wrong speed. A few minutes later, the OOD called back.

"Captain," he said, "we checked. The entire ventilation system is lined up correctly."

I thanked him, but *something* was still wrong. I got up, dressed, and walked around the ship, re-checking the ventilation system. The Officer of the Deck was correct – everything was as it should be.

I happened to walk past a piece of equipment known as the central air monitoring system, or CAMS. The CAMS had five separate electronic channels, monitoring gasses like carbon dioxide, oxygen, refrigerant gasses, etc., in the air we breathed. One of the gauges on the front panel depicted the pressure in the boat. It read 860 mm-Hg. Normal atmospheric pressure, which I *should* have seen, was 760 mm-Hg. The pressure in the boat was too high. We had too much air. Could that account for the unusual sound of the ventilation system?

Submarines have four storage banks for high pressure air. Each bank has several storage bottles that are mounted in the ballast tanks, which are filled with sea water when the boat is submerged. Three

103

banks are reserved for emergencies, and one is normally placed "on service" to supply low pressure air for various uses throughout the boat. This bank will gradually bleed down as air is used, and we would charge it back up with the air compressors about once a day. We usually ran the compressors during a normal ventilation period, when we were open to the outside environment. This way, the compressors had a plentiful source of air, and the pressure in the boat stayed at "atmospheric".

When we left California and turned north, the sea gradually became colder. The water in the ballast tanks cooled, and the air pressure in the storage bottles came down slightly. The Chief of the Watch would notice these slight drops, and he would place the offending banks "on service" during an air charge. The bank pressure would build back to normal, and the compressors would be secured. We didn't realize it, but over several weeks, we were jamming more air into the banks, although their pressures stayed normal, due to the cooler water.

Then we entered warmer water. By then, we were also in an operational environment where we could not raise a mast to ventilate. That is, we had to remain deep and totally "self-contained." As the ballast tank water warmed, the pressure in the air banks started creeping up, so the Chief of the Watch would put an offender "on service" for a few hours, and its pressure would gradually return to normal. Since we could not connect to the outside world, the air (which had to go *somewhere*) gradually accumulated in the boat's internal atmosphere. Over several weeks, this accounted for the higher pressure in the boat. We had too much air. The ventilation blowers were "complaining" because they were being forced to pump air that was considerably more dense that that for which they had been designed!

How could we get rid of the excess air? For operational reasons, we couldn't simply raise the ventilation mast above the surface and open a valve. Additionally, although we now had 860 mm-Hg of pressure in the boat, the automatic oxygen bleed system had been keeping the partial pressure of oxygen at 140 mm-Hg – right where it belonged.

Thus, the air we were breathing was only about sixteen percent oxygen (140 / 860 = ~16%). Because the partial pressure of oxygen was still correct, our bodies were perfectly happy. But if we suddenly opened a hatch and let the pressure blow down to normal, the partial pressure of oxygen would drop also. Calculations showed that it would drop below 125 mm-Hg, and that was dangerously low. Some watchstanders could pass out at that level.

We needed a way to *gradually* get rid of the air, a way that would allow the oxygen bleed system time to keep the partial pressure of oxygen at the proper level.

We started calculating. We computed that if we blew high pressure air from the storage banks into the ballast tanks for the right length of time, we would "lose" the proper amount of air. Then, we could run the air compressors and charge the banks back up. This process would be slow enough that the oxygen bleed system could "keep up". If we calculated correctly, the atmosphere in the boat would be just right – 760 mm-Hg – when the air banks were again fully charged.

But blowing air into the ballast tanks would bring us to the surface, which we could not allow.

We picked a dark night, went deep, and opened the ballast tank vents. We increased our speed so that we could hold the boat down with the diving planes. We conducted a normal blow of the ballast tanks for the proper length of time and let the air escape. It bubbled unseen to the dark surface of the sea above us.

We commenced an air charge, and the sound of the ventilation system slowly returned to normal.

I breathed a little easier.

Depth Transmitter

How deep ARE we, now?

Knowing how deep a submarine is at a given moment is important. Emergency procedures may be different, and many pieces of equipment (sonar systems, for example) have settings that depend on a submarine's depth. We <u>could</u> install depth gauges throughout the boat, but that would require many hull penetrations or lots of sea pressure piping. These are not good things. ("Keep the water out of the people tank.")

Accordingly, modern submarines have a system that measures sea pressure (depth) with one hull penetration and a short run of small piping. The equipment then transmits this information *electrically* to wherever it's needed. One day, our system stopped working, and we <u>had</u> to fix it.

How this system measures sea pressure and converts this information to an electrical signal is an important part of this story, so just grit your teeth and read on ...

The depth transmitter is a box about one and a half feet on a side. It is located in a corner of the Control Room. A small pipe (tubing, actually) connects the box to a hull valve, and electrical cabling disappears into a wire bundle. Inside, there is a bellows with a divider plate down the middle. Sea water under submergence pressure is on one side of the divider, pushing on the plate. On the other side of the plate, a spring on a screw pushes on the plate in the opposite direction, opposing the sea pressure. A position sensor notes when the divider plate moves off "center".

The sensor sends a signal to a motor, and the motor turns the spring-screw assembly to reposition the divider plate back in the "center". The number of turns the motor-spring-screw assembly has to turn is a measure of how hard the system has to "work" to oppose the sea pressure on the other side if the divider plate. That is, the number of turns is a measure of depth.

The motor we are talking about was a special kind (called a "synchro motor", but you don't really care – right?). Unlike motors that turn and turn, a synchro motor only turns a little, and then stops. When it operated properly, ours would stop as soon as the sensor noted that the divider plate was back in the "center".

This is a basic kind of control system. It seeks a "null" (the divider plate getting to the center) and then stops. A control system often has another input, called negative velocity input, to improve stability. Such an input *opposes* the position error signal. It says, "Slow down. You're going too fast." (Imagine a base runner trying to steal second. If he's going too fast as he approaches the bag, he risks overshooting. He knows he has to slow down, so he slides.)

In a control system like our depth transmitter, the "negative velocity feedback" comes from a set of windings in the synchro motor. When the motor is turning rapidly, these windings have a voltage signal. This voltage is used to slow the motor as it gets close to the null position. It was these windings that failed, somewhere inside the motor.

The result was an unstable system. The motor went back and forth, several times a second, trying to get to the null. Worse, all the depth readouts, throughout the boat, dutifully followed along, spinning rapidly back and forth. In normal operation, these counters moved slowly, as the submarine changed depth. They were never designed to spin rapidly and continuously, and we knew they would soon fail.

We soon found out that we did not have a replacement motor in spares. We did find a fire-control synchro that was electrically identical, but it was the size of a thimble. The one we needed was the size of a five-pound coffee can. It was obvious that the tiny fire-control synchro motor could never turn the spring – screw assembly.

But the fire-control synchro motor _did_ have intact velocity windings. So we wired the two synchro motors in parallel, but used the feedback windings of the fire-control synchro. Our old motor was strong enough to turn the screw, while the fire-control motor (which followed along slavishly, pushing nothing) provided the feedback.

Worked like a charm!

Heading South

Underway repair of the rudder ram

PARCHE left Charleston behind, and we sailed through the Panama Canal to our new home port in the Pacific. We would be at Mare Island Naval Shipyard, in Vallejo, just north of San Francisco. It was a little unusual to be home-ported at a shipyard, but having the yard's industrial facilities close at hand would be essential to our new mission.

We arrived at Mare Island, and we began what was to be a year-long conversion to our new oceanographic research configuration. The ship was almost brand new (we were then the newest submarine in the Pacific Fleet) and most of our equipment would not be modified, but the oceanographic additions were extensive, and we settled down for a long period in the yard.

I had been the Supply Officer on SCAMP, and I had developed a deep appreciation for the value of a sound spare parts posture. Having the spares was essential, of course, but you also had to have an administrative organization that could tell you what spares you had for a given equipment, how many you had, and where they were stowed on the ship. Knowing we would be in the yard for many months, I requested and received funding for a SOAP overhaul.

SOAP was the supply operations assistance program. In a SOAP overhaul, all of the ship's spares were taken out of their lockers and moved to a warehouse on the yard. Each spare part was inspected and inventoried. At the same time, every piece of equipment on the ship was inventoried. This last information would be combined with a list of new equipment to guarantee that every on-board system was properly supported.

All the data were then mailed to the Naval Supply Center in Mechanics-burg, Pennsylvania. The Supply Center computers matched the spares we already had with the equipment that was on board. We then received lists of what we needed, what we had that was extra, new manuals, and new index cards. We requested funds to order what we needed, and submitted the requisitions to the supply system.

At that time, for funding reasons, the Navy was trying to reduce the number of spares that a ship was required to carry. If the fleet usage data showed that a part seldom failed, a replacement was no longer required to be carried in on-board spares on every ship. The part would still be stocked in supply centers, at shipyards, or on submarine tenders. If you already had some of these items, expensive parts could be turned in to the supply system for credit. Inexpensive items were to be discarded.

My pack-rat instincts came to the fore. I could understand not buying parts that seldom failed, and I could understand turning in expensive spares that someone else might need, but I could not accept simply throwing away a perfectly good part, just because it had not been needed often in the past. So, I told the men of the SOAP team that no part was to be discarded without my expressed approval, and I scheduled time at the warehouse to review the proposed discards.

I did not disagree with the new policy, but I could not bring myself to throw away a part just because it was inexpensive when I might need it some day. I used the requirement for extraordinary reliability that was associated with our new mission to justify my position. Even so, I was scolded by the Force Supply Department for undermining the new policy. The Admiral, familiar with my mission, supported me, and the uproar subsided.

One of the packages destined for the trash was a padded envelope about ten inches square. It was labeled, "Ring, packing, chevron, one each." It cost about six dollars. A little research revealed that it was a packing ring for the rudder ram. Although I had never heard of a rudder ram packing failure, I tossed the envelope into the "keep" pile.

(You can probably see where this is going, but read on. It gets better!)

Now, fast forward two years. We were transiting under the ice, and I received a call from the Officer of the Deck.

"Captain, we have a problem. We have a leak on the rudder ram that sprays oil in the engine room whenever we turn the rudder to the right," was his report.

"Very well", I replied. "Put the rudder amidships, bring the ship to a hover, and call the Engineer. I'll be right up."

The rudder ram is a closed cylinder about six feet long and a foot in diameter. Inside, a spool moves right and left in response to oil being ported into the ends of the cylinder. A smooth metal rod (the "actuator") is attached to the spool and extends out one end of the ram cylinder. A ring of chevron[32] packing surrounds the rod where it passes through the end of the cylinder. This packing forms a seal that keeps the oil inside the ram cylinder. A linkage connects the rod to the rudder. When the spool and the rod move back and forth, the rudder turns right and left. It was the seal ring on the actuator rod that had failed, and it had to be replaced.

The Engineer, Frank Stewart, assessed the problem and made his report.

"It doesn't look good, Captain. We'll have to disassemble the ram to slide a new packing ring over the end of the actuator rod, and I'm not sure we have a spare ring. We're checking now."

"Don't worry, Frank. We've got one", I said.

(The Engineer wondered how I knew, but then the Captain knows all, right?)

We located the spare ring. We stayed in our hover for eighteen hours, while the engineers disassembled the ram, installed the new packing, and restored the system. We tested it – no leaks – and we were soon underway, making up for lost time.

Later, one of the junior petty officers caught up with me as I passed through the Crew's Mess.

---

[32] If you cut a ring of chevron packing, and look at the cut end, it looks like a "V" or chevron , hence the name. In use, oil presses one arm of the "V" against the fixed cylinder cap, and the other arm against the moving rod.

"Captain," he said. "We didn't need to worry. Up here, all directions are 'south', and we didn't need a rudder at all."

I had to think about that one …

Torpedo Room

An alarm is properly handled

You don't train on the big things. You emphasize the little things: the minutiae of good watchstanding, the value of a good log, the careful attention to proper procedures. You hope that when serious circumstances present themselves that a pervasive attitude of excellence will come to the fore and carry you through. Once in a while, you're right.

One quiet night on a transit, I was touring the ship. Just looking around. Toward the end of my tour, I came to the Torpedo Room.

The Torpedo Room on **PARCHE** had two entrances. The main entry was at the forward end of the room, near the torpedo tubes. A second door was at the opposite, aft end of the room. On a tour, I would normally come in the after end, walk forward, and leave though the main doorway.

Most of the room was dark, since several men were sleeping in temporary bunks alongside the torpedoes. The forward end, near the tubes and their control panel, was softly lighted. Here, the Torpedoman of the Watch monitored the tube controls and instrumentation. On this night, the TMOW was joined by a friend, and the two torpedomen were quietly talking, passing the time. Neither man realized I had entered the room.

Suddenly, the quiet was interrupted by an alarm buzzer on the Torpedo Tube Control Panel. The two men sprang into action. The watchstander silenced the alarm, and the two torpedomen began investigating the problem.

"I'll get the tech manual; you get the Chief!"

I quietly turned and walked out the after door, confident that we were in good hands.

The Next Mission

PARCHE was returning from a difficult and complex mission. We had been successful, and everyone on board knew it. (Most of the crew didn't know *exactly* what we did, but to a man, they knew it was important.) Every man had worked for months to prepare the ship, and the crew's performance underway had been superb. The men were justly proud of their accomplishment.

One of the junior messcooks stopped me just outside the galley.

"Well, Captain", he asked. "How are we going to top this one?"

I replied, "Can you keep a secret?"

The young man had more security clearances than most senior people in the Service. "Of course", he answered.

I leaned forward and whispered. "Caspian Sea."

When he finally found the crew's atlas, he learned that the Caspian Sea, while admittedly large (more than 140,000 square miles) and deep (more than 1000 feet), is an entirely land-locked lake in south-western Asia.

Dark and Quiet

A drill that turned out to be much more

During an operational mission, submarines seldom conduct complex engineering drills. The requirements for stealth and plant reliability are paramount. Drills are noisy, and the reliability posture of the plant is obviously reduced when we deliberately impose even simulated casualties.[33] Training goes forward, of course, but the training is often limited to lectures, seminars, quiet walk-throughs and practice evolutions that are the foundations of a successful training program.

Once a mission is completed and the submarine returns to waters closer to home, however, the gloves come off. On **PARCHE**, we usually scheduled a series of dedicated engineering training days near the end of each mission. The syllabus for the period gradually progressed from simple "warm-up" drills to complicated situations that demanded response from the entire crew.

The schedule itself was unusual. Normally, the **PARCHE** (like most US submarines) mans six-hour watches. Most of the crew prefers them, even though four watches a day require that a three-section watch bill rotate. When we scheduled a dedicated training period, we split each day into three four-hour drill periods and two six-hour rest periods. There were three watch sections. At any given time, one

---

[33] We often heard, "It ain't a drill no more, when the rods hit the bottom." The "rods" are the reactor control rods, and the saying refers to "scramming" - shutting down the reactor.

section would be on watch, one would have just gone off, and the third (scheduled for the next watch) was designated to assist the on-duty section in the event of a casualty.

Having five watch periods in a day makes for a complex rotation, but over a three day period, everything evens out, and each section has the same number of watches in the same time slots. (You can work this out on paper!) The sequence was fatiguing, and after three days we would all be ready for a rest, but the crew actually enjoyed the change from the daily routine and I think they enjoyed the challenges of the drills.

Conducting a drill was an evolution in itself. We used a system of colored ball caps to identify the drill team. Blue hats were worn by the drill initiators, who would impose the simulated casualty. These were the men who would (for example) trip a breaker or shut a valve to initiate a drill. Red hats were worn by the safety monitors, who would guarantee that a certain plant parameter was not exceeded, or that a particular action was (or was not) taken. They would only step in if necessary – as far as the on-watch section was concerned, they were "not there". Finally, the "Yellow–Hats" were the drill monitors with clipboards who recorded the section's response for review and discussion later.

Each drill was briefed beforehand, normally in the wardroom. The method of initiation was discussed, safety observers were given their assignments, and the drill monitors decided what to watch for. Mistakes we had made on the same drill in the past were discussed in detail – hopefully we had learned and the mistakes would not be repeated. When all was in readiness, we would head into the engineering spaces, where the on-watch section would try to estimate the complexity of the coming drill by the number of red hats observed among the drill team.

The day of this story was the last day of a three-day sequence. We were on the last watch section, and this was to be their last drill. As I mentioned, the drills got progressively more complex and demanding as we worked through the sequence, so everyone knew that this last drill was going to be a big one. Little did we know ...

For complex evolutions where the entire ship was likely to be involved, my Executive Officer, Archie Clemins,[34] and I would normally arrange to be in different places. One of us would be in the Control Room, forward, and the other was usually in the Maneuvering Room, aft. This was simply a safety precaution. We each knew "what was coming", and we could easily step in if necessary. The Engineer Officer, Frank Stewart, was usually in Maneuvering also, though he could position himself anywhere in the engineering plant if the "action" was to be somewhere else.

At this point, it is helpful to discuss a little submarine design philosophy. Modern submarines are complex installations, with many separate pieces of equipment and machinery. Almost all components require alternating current (AC) electrical power, and this electricity is usually generated by steam-driven turbine generators powered by the reactor. A diesel generator can supply a limited amount of power in an emergency.

---

[34] Archie Clemins was perhaps the finest naval officer I ever knew. He was to become Commander in Chief of the Pacific Fleet, with the four stars of an Admiral. I was fortunate to serve with him.

A system of redundant electrical busses distributes the power to installations throughout the ship. Some equipment is run when needed (like air compressors), some is optional but normally run continuously (like ventilation blowers), and some is required all the time (like lighting, vital oil pumps, and most instrumentation). The electrical busses are designated "vital" or "non-vital" depending on the installations they power and the reliability of the busses themselves.

Automatic bus transfer switches are used in several places to transfer loads, when required, from a bus that has gone dead to one that still has power. Redundancy is piled on redundancy. No matter how complex the drill, or how severe the actual casualty, the electric distribution system is designed to guarantee that the vital loads *always* have power. Normally, this works perfectly. It is probably accurate to say that none of us, myself included, had *ever* seen a nuclear submarine without *any* AC power, whether at sea, in port, or in drydock.[35] Until,...

One last technical detail: We *never* started the reactor after an automatic shutdown without knowing what had caused the failure (and repairing it, of course). In a drill where we manually scrammed[36] the reactor, this meant that the watch section could not restart the reactor until they "found" why it had shut down. Thus, the drill initiators could impose a recovery delay simply by withholding information. The drill scenarios often dictated this to drive the watch section into complex configurations.

---

[35] Even in drydock, we *always* guaranteed power to reactor instrumentation. "The reactor never sleeps ..."

[36] A "scram" is a reactor shutdown where some or all control rods are rapidly inserted into the reactor core, shutting down the chain reaction.

For this drill, we had planned just such an obstacle. The watch section would not be able to initially determine the "cause of the scram", and they would have to configure the plant for a long delay in recovery. The objective of the drill was the development of skill in exactly this reconfiguration process. The watch section would have to shed electrical loads and busses until they ended up with one small, but very vital, bus.

When the Engineer decided everyone was ready, he initiated the drill. The reactor was scrammed, and propulsion power to the main engine was lost. The Diving Officer, by procedure, began coasting up to a shallower depth, perfecting his trim as the boat slowed. As expected, the watch section was unable to determine why the reactor had shut down, and they reported that "the recovery would be delayed". They began to reconfigure the electric distribution system to save power.

Every Commanding Officer and every Officer of the Deck has a set of favorite electric bus indicators somewhere in the Control Room. The indicator may be a "pump running" light on a panel, or it may be the sound of a particular ventilation fan. Using "his" indicators, an OOD can tell which busses still have power even before a formal report comes from the Engineering Officer of the Watch. I used "my" set, and I was able to follow the expected sequence of bus de-energization as the drill proceeded.

Then, the last, vital bus went dead. You didn't need a set of special indicators: everything was dark and quiet.

The reactor fully shut down, with all the control rods fully in. All coolant flow stopped. All the instrumentation that we used to monitor the reactor plant, and every other system on the ship, went dark.

I had seen blackness this absolute once before, when a Ranger deep in Carlsbad Caverns warned us, and then briefly turned off the lights. Throughout the Control Room, indicator and status lights, normally always energized, were dark[37]. And everything was quiet. Running motors, ventilation fans and blowers, even the little cooling fans in individual pieces of electronic equipment, all coasted to a stop.

Tension in the Control Room was high. As I have said, none of us had ever been in this situation before and I knew (if we could have seen them!) that there were some "wide eyes". I was scheduled to be relieved in a month or so, and the crew was aware of the coming change of command. I announced into the quiet darkness, "You guys are just doing this to test me, right?" The tension evaporated.

Actually, it was not completely quiet: Several electronic cabinets had small, battery-powered alarms that sounded a warning tone when normal power to the equipment was lost. Until we could find these units (in the dark!) and silence the alarms, we had to endure several high-pitched whistles coming at us from several directions.[38]

We formally secured the drill – we now had a real casualty situation on our hands. I did not know what had happened in

---

[37] We quickly broke out emergency flashlights and battery-powered lanterns were turned on, so we soon had rudimentary lighting.

[38] For technical reasons, a pure, single-frequency tone is *very* difficult to locate. Our ears are badly confused by "side-lobes" that seem to be coming from a different spot. This is the same phenomenon that is involved in the design of directional antennas.

Maneuvering, but I knew the Engineer and the Executive Officer were there. I was confident they were doing what was necessary to restore power, and the *last* thing they needed was my asking, "What happened?" In the Control Room, I had other things to do.

We would have to go to periscope depth to get air to run the diesel. We needed electrical power, and it was obvious the turbine generators would not be able to supply power for some time. I needed to conserve enough hydraulic fluid to raise one periscope and ensure the area was clear.[39] My first order was, "Planes and rudder on zero, and leave them there." No sense wasting hydraulic fluid on trying to maintain course or an exact depth. We eased up to periscope depth and raised a periscope. The afternoon was bright; the ocean was clear.[40]

Within a couple of minutes, the engineers restored one vital bus, and we took advantage of power to the valve actuators to put an air bubble in the ballast tanks. This caused us to wallow on the surface, with the decks awash. More importantly, it raised the diesel induction above the surface of the sea, without having to raise the induction mast. Now, all we had to do was start the diesel, and we would have a little power.

I called our best diesel operator, a Chief Machinist's Mate, the leading petty officer of the Auxiliary Division, to the Control Room.

"Chief," I said. "We *have* to get the diesel on line. Go down to the diesel compartment, but do not take over. Let the Auxiliaryman of the

---

[39] The hydraulic system "stores" a small amount of pressurized oil in a set of accumulators. The system will function, for a short while, without power.
[40] We were far at sea and not near any shipping lanes.

Watch do his job, just the way he has trained. Your role is to break out the procedure, and follow down the steps, just to make sure he doesn't forget anything. Treat it like a routine monitored evolution."

The Chief acknowledged the order and departed for the diesel compartment. The engine was started perfectly, first time.

We connected the diesel generator onto the electrical distribution system and we loaded it to about 90% of its capacity. (No sense in pushing the limit!) We now had a little bit of power, and we could begin the painstaking process of bringing the submarine back to life.

The Electrical Plant Control Panel operator who had caused the problem by opening the wrong breaker was convinced that he would be disqualified on the spot. He was one of our finest electricians, but he had made a grievous error. Instead, he was told, "You got us into this. You're staying on that panel until we get out." His grin made it clear that this was the correct order.[41]

The Engineer came forward with a new problem. Before we commenced the drill, we had had steam in all the turbines and in all the steam piping. Those components were obviously hot. Now, with no ventilation or air conditioning (the diesel generator could not carry those electrical loads), the engineering spaces were heating up. Rising temperatures would soon make the entire engineering plant uninhabitable.

We broke out the diagrams, and we found an unusual way to rearrange the ventilation dampers. By flowing air *backwards* through

---

[41] This electrician later came to our critique in the Crew's Mess with a paper bag, complete with eyeholes, over his head. He had inscribed the bag, "The Unknown Electrician."

some of the lines, we could bring outside air in through the induction and dump it in the engine room. Then, we aligned the diesel to take its suction on the ship's atmosphere instead of the induction. We opened all the interior watertight doors, and dragged the (now heated) air into the diesel, where it was consumed and exhausted overboard. Temperatures in the engineering spaces started to come down.

By now, we were about an hour into the casualty. We were snorkeling on the diesel, and we had enough electrical power to get by. We had control of our depth, and there were no ship contacts in sight. The engineers were calibrating the instrumentation in preparation for starting the reactor. We were making good progress.

I turned to the Officer of the Deck and asked, "Do you have the picture?" He replied that he did.

"Fine", I said. "I'm going to bed. Call me if you have a problem."

The OOD swallowed his surprise, but he acknowledged. I went into my stateroom and lay down, but I didn't go to sleep. (!)

By eavesdropping on the sound-powered-phone circuit, and by listening to the periodic reports the Engineering Officer of the Watch would make to the Officer of the Deck over an announcing circuit, I was able to keep track of our progress, without seeming to be involved. For major steps, the OOD would come to me for permission or to report a significant accomplishment.[42] Everything proceeded smoothly. Five hours after we started the drill, we were back at full power, making flank speed.

---

[42] For example, "Request permission to take the reactor critical" or "Captain, the electrical plant is in a full power lineup. Request permission to secure the diesel."

Epilogue I

After a casualty of this magnitude, it was essential that we inform our Squadron Commander in San Diego and the Commander of Pacific Fleet Submarines (ComSubPac) in Pearl Harbor. As soon as we could break radio silence, we transmitted a short summary. We knew, however, that ComSubPac was in the air, flying from Honolulu to meet us in San Francisco. He would not see the message before coming aboard.

When the Admiral came aboard from the tug, just inside the Golden Gate, he joined me on the bridge. I handed him a copy of the message, saying, "Admiral, you need to read this right away." The Admiral read the message and then replaced it in the envelope. He put the envelope into his pocket, saying, "I'm glad to see you are not forgetting to train on these missions." He made no further comment and the drill was not discussed again.

Epilogue II

Years later, a crewman from **PARCHE** found my name on the **PARCHE** web-site and sent an e-mail greeting. We corresponded, and I proudly told the story of the Auxiliaryman who had played such a crucial part by starting the diesel in difficult circumstances.

MM2 (SS) Roy Becker responded: "I was Aux of the Watch."

Small world. Good people.

Epilogue III

I shared this story with the Engineer, Frank Stewart, at the 2004 PARCHE decommissioning. Frank related to me that he had also lost all AC power when he commanded his own submarine, the USS LOUISVILLE, years later. Although the circumstances were a little different, the blackness was equally dark.

The Double Doors

"What do you mean, 'You've lost an ensign?'"

The missions on **PARCHE** owed their success to many people. The crew, of course, was extraordinary, but any Commanding Officer will say that. The families were more vital than they knew (but any Commanding officer will say *that*, too). **PARCHE** also had a huge cadre of dedicated people who worked, unheralded, behind the scenes. The men and women of the Mare Island Naval Shipyard provided their skills day in and day out, for months and years on end. (It was often said that these folks only *lent* us their boat to take to sea. There was more than a smidgen of truth in this statement.)

The Naval Staffs in San Diego and Pearl Harbor, many of whom were never privy to our mission – security compartmentation was vital – added their expertise. Military and civilian personnel in Washington – in the Pentagon and in other branches of the government – guaranteed that we had the resources we needed. Every one of these individuals contributed. Without them, we could not have succeeded.

After every mission, the Commanding Officer would conduct a series of briefings in Honolulu and Washington on the trip just concluded. The objective of this "road show" was to provide the cleared people with some indication of what their efforts had accomplished. In addition, a clearer understanding of the situations we encountered enabled those same people to better plan for the next mission.

I usually had one of the junior officers from the wardroom accompany me on these trips. My purpose was threefold: the trip was a partial "reward" for a job well done, and the JO was able to help with the logistics of the trip. Most importantly, he would bring back to the crew an appreciation of how well our mission had been received at senior levels in the government. (It was *expected* that the CO would say, "They loved it." When one of "their own" provided the details, well, that was *really* something.)

On one such trip, I was accompanied by Ensign Curtis Murphy. Curt was one of the finest young officers I ever served with. He was enthusiastic, professionally competent, and he was liked and respected by everyone. His perpetual good humor made him a natural for the "horse-holder" role on the road.

In a sense, our Program Office in the Pentagon didn't exist. Although it guided and supported virtually every aspect of our operations, it kept a very low profile. It was not in any Pentagon office directory, and its telephone numbers were unlisted. The Office was hidden behind two sets of nondescript double security doors in the Pentagon "hinterlands". Visitors called ahead, were met at the doors, and escorted all the time they were inside. Cleared personnel were free to move about, once inside, but we still knew that certain parts of the facility were "off limits".

On this trip, Curt dropped me at an entrance to the Pentagon, and drove off to park the rental car. (Open parking at the Pentagon was a *long* way away.) I walked up to the Program Office to prepare for the day's briefing schedule. Shortly after I arrived, I realized that Curt had never been to the office before. He did not know where it was.

As a commissioned officer, Curt would have no trouble entering the Pentagon itself, but once inside he would be out of luck. Inquiries to the Pentagon security officers would bring only friendly shrugs. Office directories would be no help. Telephone books would have no entries. Someone would have to find Curt and bring him to the office. And only I knew him – no-one else knew what he looked like.

To make matters worse, we had no way of knowing where he would find a parking place. We therefore did not know what Pentagon entrance he would use. We would have to "cover" them all. We would have to send a staff member to each probable entrance with instructions to find a bewildered ensign, identify him, and escort him to the Program Office. We divided up the possibilities, and then headed for the double doors, ready to fan out and head for the Pentagon entrances.

We opened the doors, and there was Curt Murphy, telephone in hand, calling inside for access. "How did you find this place?" we asked.

"It was easy," he replied. "I just asked a secretary."

Epilogue

I shared this story with Curt Murphy in my 2004 Christmas card. He added a detail that I had long forgotten. In his words:

Prior to leaving the car, you gave the "office" phone number to me with instructions to call for directions when I arrived at an entrance. I called... only to find that phone number which you provided happened to ring at the local Chinese laundry! I have often wondered if that was a legitimate mistake, operational training, or a perverse sense of humor at work.

Drydocks and Archie

Her oceanic research mission required frequent modifications to PARCHE, and we went into drydock at the Mare Island Naval Shipyard six times during my tour. This was not all bad. It afforded me and my officers with a type of shiphandling training that we could never have received anywhere else.

When a submarine was to go into drydock at Mare Island, she normally spent a week or so at her normal berth, getting ready. The reactor was shut down and cooled; scaffolding was erected topside, and the shipyard workers got a head start on some of their jobs that did not require the ship to be high and dry.

When the day came to enter the dock, the submarine was a five thousand ton inert hulk that could not move under her own power. Three shipyard tugs would arrive for the move. They would be securely attached to the submarine, as follows:

Two powerful tugs were made up alongside, with their centerlines parallel to the submarine's centerline. The forward tug would point aft, while the after tug would point forward. The third tug, normally smaller, would come in between the two large tugs, perpendicular to the centerlines, pointed straight into the submarine's side.

Got it? (It doesn't really matter. The bottom line is that with the proper engine and rudder orders to the proper tug, you could make the whole assembly go forward, backward, turn on a dime, or move sideways. It really was quite elegant.)

One other factor is important. Because we were home-ported at the shipyard and frequently came in and went out, we got to know the shipyard pilots (who controlled the tugs) quite well. More importantly, the shipyard pilots got to know us. Eventually, the Senior Shipyard Pilot allowed us to actually control the tugs as we moved the submarine from her berth and up the river to the drydock. (The Pilot would "take over" just before we actually entered the dock.) This was an exceptional opportunity, and we were most appreciative of the trust placed in us.

In practice, my Officer of the Deck would send helm and engine orders to each tug on a hand-held radio. The tug would acknowledge with a short toot of its whistle and then execute the order. The Senior Pilot and I would stand by the Officer of the Deck, ready to step in if he got into trouble. The really difficult part for me (and I'm sure, for the Pilot) was to remain silent and let the young officer do it "his way" when we could see a slightly better order.

One of a Naval Officer's most important jobs is to train his relief. (You don't see this as much in civilian industry, where the man you train too well may take *your* job!) I had to train my Executive Officer, Archie Clemins, for the day when he would command his own ship[43]. For our last entry into drydock during my tour, I decided that Archie should be the supervisor at the Officer of the Deck's side, ready to intercede if needed. Archie would remain silent if the trip up the river

---

[43] This was not a difficult chore. Archie Clemins was *sharp*. He later wore an admiral's four stars as the Commander in Chief of the Pacific Fleet, so I must have trained him well.

proceeded well. I would be topside, on the sail scaffolding, aft and out of the way.

I could observe our progress, but with the diesel engine operating to provide emergency power, *I could not hear* the orders that the Officer of the Deck was sending to the tugs. I could hear the tugs' answering toots, of course, but I could not hear the helm and engine orders they were about to execute. Realistically, I could not intercede if the young officer sent a tug a dangerous order. That was Archie's job.

The trip up the river proceeded fine. Archie was able to remain silent, letting the Officer of the Deck control everything. Just before we crossed the sill to enter the dock, the young officer handed the radio to the Senior Pilot, and the pilot expertly moved us into position over the drydock blocks.

Afterwards, Archie came to me. "Captain", he said, "that was the hardest thing I've ever had to do."

Coming alongside

"Nobody does it better ..."

Most submarine evolutions, for obvious reasons, cannot be observed from *outside* the submarine. When **USS PARCHE** occasionally arrived at the submarine base in San Diego (our normal home port was at a shipyard near San Francisco), we were watched carefully. The squadron staff officers would line up on the tender to observe our performance. Each man was convinced that *his* old ship could do it better. We wanted to prove them all wrong.

Submarines usually use four mooring lines, numbered from "one" at the bow to "four" near the stern. Numbers "two" and "three" are amidships, in an **X** configuration: Line "two" tends aft, and "three" angles forward. Lines "one" and "four" hold the bow and stern (respectively) close to the pier, while "two" and "three" keep the boat from surging ahead or back.

On **PARCHE**, we used a system of two-part hand signals to control the lines. The Officer of the Deck on the bridge would direct an order to a particular line by holding up one, two, three or four fingers, followed by a motion conveying the order he wanted. "Put over" was a forearm throwing motion. "Slack" was a rocking motion, palm down. "Hold" was a fist.

All orders were duplicated to the men on deck using a sound-powered telephone. The "sound man" on deck would repeat-back the order to make sure it had been received properly, but if it was already being properly carried out (because of the hand signal), he would do no more. An experienced man (a Chief or senior petty officer) would be in charge on deck, but normally he didn't have to do or say anything. No-one on deck hollered a greeting to a friend on the pier, or even spoke. The evolution was quiet and professional.

Each mooring line position had a light line as well as the mooring hawser. One end of the line had a weighted bolo that could be thrown to the pier. The other end was tied to the hawser, so that the heavier hawser could be pulled ashore.

After a mooring line was looped over a bollard on the pier, the man in charge of that line on the submarine would pull in the slack and take a turn on the cleat. If the submarine moved closer to the pier, he would take in slack. If the submarine eased away, he would "check" the line (apply tension to slow the ship's movement, but without breaking the hawser). All this was done automatically – he didn't have to be told. In an emergency, he could be ordered to "hold" the line, but this was seldom necessary.

Because of her research mission, **PARCHE** had powerful thrusters fore and aft that could be used to push the ship sideways. The thrusters were below the waterline and not visible from the pier. Most staff officers didn't know they were there. They attributed any occasional sideways motion to our line-handling skill, and we never told them otherwise.

PARCHE would also routinely lower all masts when making a mooring. The periscopes, radar, and radio masts would descend into the sail and be hidden from view. (A periscope was used by the navigation team when coming up the channel, but navigation was no longer necessary when alongside the pier.) The overall effect was of a smooth, lean, quiet, *professional* ship easing into her berth.

Like the song says, "Nobody does it better ..."

Your Ship, Captain

After I left command of **PARCHE**, I was stationed on the staff of a submarine squadron in San Diego. One of my duties was to periodically ride each of the squadron submarines to see how it was being operated and maintained. These "rides" were essentially informal inspections that enabled the Squadron Commander to keep his finger on the pulse of the boats under his command.

A boat scheduled for a week of training operations in local waters was an ideal candidate for such a visit. The "rider" would go aboard as the boat prepared to get underway on Monday morning and depart when she returned Friday afternoon. During the week, he would observe the boat's operations, preparing a letter report of his observations as the week progressed. Before leaving, as a courtesy to the ship's Commanding Officer, most riders would share the observations with him, adding any suggestions that came from the rider's own experience.

A senior rider was in a somewhat unusual position during these visits. He was often the Deputy Squadron Commander, and he was invariably senior to the ship's Captain, having been a Commanding Officer himself in a previous tour. But there was never any question who was the Captain of the ship. This distinction was soundly rooted in Navy Regulations, and in centuries of naval tradition, and it was clearly understood by every man aboard. The squadron deputy was treated with respect and courtesy, but he was clearly a visitor. He might make suggestions (normally only to the Captain), but he would be unlikely to give a direct order, and virtually never to a member of the ship's crew.

One week, I conducted such an inspection ride on a submarine in our squadron. Shortly after midnight, midweek, the submarine was repositioning within its assigned operating area in anticipation of more training drills later that morning. We had been assigned an area northwest of San Diego, but inside (east of) the Channel Islands off Los Angeles. (Remember that song, "Twenty-six miles across the sea,…"?) It was about two in the morning, and most of the crew was turned in. I lay in a borrowed bunk, but something was wrong, and I couldn't sleep.

I could feel the quiet vibration characteristic of a high speed transit. The engineering plant was clearly configured for maximum speed, and we were obviously at "ahead, flank". Because even a gentle change in direction of the ship results in a slight heel, it was also obvious that we were moving in a straight line. I could not sense which direction we were headed (I'm not *that* good!) but it was apparent we weren't turning. I lay there, calculating … .

I knew, roughly, the size and shape of our assigned operating area. I knew, roughly, how fast we were going. I knew we were not turning. It didn't take complicated calculations to realize that we would soon run out of our assigned area. Worse, just outside our operating area, to the west, were the Channel Islands. Breakfast on Santa Catalina is delightful; I'm sure, but not when you arrive, unexpectedly, by submarine.

I climbed out of the bunk and wandered up to a quiet, orderly, dimly lit Control Room. I glanced at the chart, and it showed that we had a few more miles of our area ahead of us, with the Channel Islands slightly beyond the area boundary. If our position was correctly shown on the chart, we had no problem, even as we sped ahead. We would have to slow down before long, but for the moment we appeared to be safe.

But how accurate was that position on the chart? How long had it been since we had last fixed our position? How accurate were the speed and direction instruments we were relying upon to update our position estimates? Were the soundings correct, or was the bottom rushing up to meet us? When was the Officer of the Deck planning to slow, come to periscope depth, and fix his position? I was reluctant to step in, but we might have been in an extremely dangerous position. I had just made up my mind to suggest a fix to the Officer of the Deck when I heard him order, "Ahead two thirds. Make your depth one five zero feet." He was slowing and coming shallow, preparing to come up and get a fix. The danger, if there ever was one, had passed.

For the next two hours, while the crew went about their normal routines, I looked at charts, qualification and watchbill assignments, logbooks, and navigation department administrative records. I took numerous notes, and then returned to the wardroom and broke out a pad of lined paper. I started to write.

The Submarine Force has a process to disseminate lessons learned from accidents or errors, such as a fire or an unintentional grounding. A message is drafted at the Submarine Force headquarters in Pearl Harbor and sent to every boat and command. The message outlines the mistakes that led to the accident, and then it orders the steps to prevent recurrence. These messages always begin with the clause, "Recently, a ship of this force ..." These six words have taken on an identity of their own. No-one wants to be the subject of a "recently, a ship of this force" message.

On the pad of blank paper in the wardroom, I drafted such a message. It was fictitious, of course, since there had been no accident – we had not run aground. However, when I had reviewed the Navigation Department operation and administration, I had uncovered *many* errors. In my dummy message, I listed the errors I had found as if they had been contributors to an actual grounding. (Most major accidents result from many mistakes, each of which has to line up in exactly the *wrong* way.) In order to make my fictitious ship go aground, I had to add one error that I had *not* observed. This single fiction was hidden among more than a dozen problems that I *had* seen.

By then, it was 0500, and the Commanding Officer of the ship joined me in the empty wardroom and poured two cups of coffee. I finished my obviously fictitious "draft" message, and passed it to the Captain for comment. He read through it completely, and then expressed the hope that it would never reflect a real submarine.

"Captain", I said. "One of those errors – and I won't tell you which one – is imaginary. Every one of the others is real, and they represent your ship as it existed at 0200 this morning."

The Captain left the wardroom quickly, and I returned to my bunk. My ride report for the Squadron Commander included the entry: "Conducted Navigation inspection. Discrepancies corrected."

Titanic

As the Commander of the Submarine Development Group in San Diego, I maintained a liaison with deep submergence personnel across the country. One of the most prominent experts was Dr. Robert Ballard, at the Woods Hole Oceanographic Institution. At the time (the mid-'80s), Dr. Ballard was readying an expedition to locate the **RMS** **TITANIC**, which had been tragically lost so many years before.

Dr. Ballard invited me to send a young officer on the cruise, and I had plenty of volunteers. My list was soon narrowed down to three fine officers from various units within the squadron. Now, I had to choose just one, knowing that the other two would be bitterly disappointed.

I chickened out. I called the three officers into my office.

"You are all ideal candidates", I said, "and I am not about to make a choice. You three must find some way to choose. I don't care if you draw straws, flip coins, or fight to the death in a ring. But within 72 hours, you three must come back with your selection."

Three days later, they came with their answer.

"We're _all_ going. There is no reason to leave _anyone_ behind. Each of our commands has said they could spare us, and Dr. Ballard could use all the help and expertise we can provide. This is a once-in-a-lifetime opportunity. We can find the travel money, somewhere."

They were right, of course. Dr. Ballard was happy to add all the men to the expedition and I was able to scrounge up *three* airline tickets to Massachusetts. We all know now that the search was successful.

Was this leadership? Probably not. But it certainly was a fine solution at the time!

No Smoking

Something had to change

After command of **PARCHE**, I was assigned to the Submarine Squadron Three staff in San Diego. As one of the squadron deputies, I would often ride the submarines in the squadron to review their performance. One of the boats was **USS GUARDFISH**, and she was one of the best.

One day, the Squadron Commander called me to his office. The commanding officer of the **GUARDFISH**, which was at that time deployed to the western Pacific, had a medical problem, and a replacement commanding officer was needed. I had been tapped.

Throw me in that briar patch. To leave a desk and go to sea again as a Commanding Officer? I was not ready to go right away, but I was in two minutes.

Ray Vaughan was the **GUARDFISH** CO. As I said, this was a fine ship, largely due to Ray's leadership. Ray was due for normal relief in about five months, and the prospective commanding officer was already in the training "pipeline". Mine would only be a short stewardship, but it sure beat driving a desk.

I took command of **USS GUARDFISH**, without fanfare, in Korea. Ray left, reluctantly, for treatment. Now I was faced with an unusual problem. The position of "commanding officer" on a US Navy ship is absolute. There is no such thing as an "interim CO" or a "temporary CO". Either you are the commanding officer, or you are not. Clean.

Straightforward. Now, GUARDFISH had a new CO, and I had to make the boat <u>mine</u>.

My situation was complicated because I knew the officers in the wardroom, the chief petty officers, and many of the crew. They had often seen me aboard as a squadron deputy. Additionally, Ray's departure was sudden and unexpected and the crew had little time to mentally prepare for the transition. Finally, as I have mentioned, Ray Vaughan was a good commanding officer, and any replacement would be viewed with reserve.

Normally, a new CO makes his presence known by changing something. The crew accepts that the "new guy" wants it done differently, and before too long the identities of the new commanding officer and the ship itself start to merge. This is as it should be. My problem was that there was not much of Ray's legacy that needed changing. The ship was well run, and I did not want to muck it up with an ill-advised change.

The solution came to me. Each section of the ship's diving party included three or four junior sailors who rotated among several control stations: the fairwater planes and rudder, the stern planes, and a messenger billet. Each watchstander manned a position for a half hour, and then rotated to the next position to prevent boredom.

While on the planes, a watchstander would often "light up", to help pass the time, I suppose. Each station had a convenient "butt kit", and most (but not all!) of the ashes made it into these containers. Smoking did not really interfere with their routine duties, but a lighted cigarette could have had a detrimental effect if immediate actions were needed in response to a casualty. (This is thin, I recognize, but I needed *something*.)

So I put out the smoking lamp on the diving stand. You should have heard the howls of protest. A whole thirty minutes without a cigarette! The seven or eight junior men involved spread the word throughout the ship. Calamity had struck, and it was not clear how we could survive.

Most of the crew, totally unaffected, viewed the whole affair with mild amusement. The crisis passed, and **GUARDFISH** had a new Commanding Officer.

Convoy

My admiral is bigger than your admiral

When I was the Commander of the Submarine Development Group in San Diego, I was tapped to arrange for the shipment of some highly classified equipment, then in storage at Pearl Harbor. I flew to Hawaii, where a packaging support team and a squad of armed guards was already assembled. A conference with the Fleet Commander testified to the importance of our effort, and it was made abundantly clear: <u>No mistakes</u>. The Admiral gave me a card with his private telephone number in case I ran into difficulties.

My team set about packaging the equipment, and a dedicated transport plane was dispatched from somewhere in the midwest to receive the shipment. The plane would land at Barbers Point Naval Air Station, and taxi to a remote corner of the tarmac. We were to deliver the crates directly to the plane.

I realized that a courtesy visit to the Commanding Officer of the air station was appropriate. I donned my whites, with all the colorful ribbons and my gold dolphins, and drove to Barbers Point. I met with the Executive Officer of the base – the CO was playing golf.

The XO was friendly and courteous, a little wary, and understandably curious.

We exchanged pleasantries, and I dropped the bomb: "I just wanted you to know that in two days I will be bringing an armed convoy through your back gate to the airstrip. Your people will not be allowed to inspect the shipment."

At the time, President Reagan was planning to fly into Honolulu, and Barbers Point was the designated alternate airstrip for Air Force One. Security at the base had been appropriately tightened. Every package, even briefcases, was being searched.

The Executive Officer was in a difficult position, and he was adamant: My request (for that's how he characterized it, though it wasn't a request at all) was "not acceptable". No-one would be bringing armed personnel and a concealed shipment onto the base. On the other hand, my instructions were equally clear: "Make it happen." We went back and forth, with me (for security reasons) unable to provide answers.

Frustrated, the Executive Officer finally stated, "No way. I'll call the Fleet Commander if I have to."

That was the wrong thing to say. I reached into my pocket and handed him the Admiral's card. "Here's the number," and I took my leave.

I don't know if the call was ever made, but the convoy met the plane and the shipment left on time.

The Blonde

The rake in Yokosuka

After command of **PARCHE** and **GUARDFISH**, and after a brief tour on the Submarine Squadron THREE staff in San Diego, I was assigned to the Strategic Studies Group in Newport, Rhode Island. There, for a year, eight fleet-experienced officers were tasked to analyze and answer the question, "If you had to go to war _now_, how would you employ the weapons and resources _that you have now_?" (That is, we were divorced from budget and procurement questions.)

(You might be surprised to learn how little time leaders have to consider that question. Unencumbered by deadlines, telephones, and IN-baskets, we were able to develop some very valuable concepts.)

At the end of the year, we summarized our analysis and prepared a presentation of our results. We split up, and carried that presentation to military and civilian leaders around the world. On one such trip, four of us were dispatched to the Far East.

We met with the Ambassador in Tokyo and made our presentation to him and his staff. Our next destination was the Yokosuka Naval Base, where we would meet with the Commander, SEVENTH Fleet. Yokosuka was only about thirty-five miles away, but that could be many hours in Tokyo traffic, so the Admiral dispatched his helicopter to the Embassy for us.

We rode in style over the sights of Tokyo and Yokohama, and landed at the heliport at the Yokosuka Naval Base. The rotors had just stopped turning when an attractive blonde stepped out from the greeting party.

The lady came up to me and we embraced. She planted a big kiss, and we exchanged hugs. I had known Anne for many years, and we were very close. Her husband was at sea, but we arranged to have dinner together, in her quarters, that evening.

My compatriots on the Studies Group made no comments, but eyebrows were raised. Who would have believed that straight-laced Jack had a girl in a foreign port? And a good-looking one to boot ...

My reputation as a rake was destined to be short lived. The next day, we were having lunch in the Submarine Officers' Mess when an old friend came in and recognized me. He came over to our table.

"Hi, Jack! Good to see you. I heard you guys were in town. I saw your sister, Anne, at the Exchange this morning, and she said she had met you when you landed at the heliport ...

The Mail Robber

Don't mess with these guys

This is a true story, told to me by a participant. It actually happened. Sometimes, security *really* was a problem. Read on ...

A Development Group submarine (not mine!) departed on a highly classified mission. An equipment failure forced a very unusual diversion to a remote site for repairs. A critical spare part was located, and the Commodore and a Project Department officer (Lieutenant Bill S., who told me this story) hand-carried the part to the ship.

While the part was being installed and tested, a decision was made to allow the crew to "write home". Procedures were established to ensure that no classified information was included, and each letter was then signed, sealed, and stamped. The letters were collected in the ship's bright orange "US MAIL" bag. Because a local postmark would provide a clue as to the mission's general direction, all the letters would be carried back to San Diego and mailed from there.

Returning home, Bill checked the mail bag and his suitcase at the airport. Seats were limited, and the Commodore told Bill to "Go ahead". The Commodore would take the next flight.

At Lindbergh Field in San Diego, Bill went to the carousel to retrieve his luggage. He had just picked up the mail bag when two strong arms pinned his. Postal Inspectors. They had been alerted by a sharp ticket agent in a distant city.

"Where did you get that bag?" "Where are you coming from?" "Why are you carrying U.S. mail?"

For security reasons, Bill couldn't (and wouldn't) say anything. Nothing. The Inspectors were _not_ amused. And the Commodore, who presumably would make everything right, wasn't due for hours. Bill wouldn't even tell the Inspectors where the Commodore was flying in from.

Parking at the old Lindbergh Field was limited, and Bill's wife was circling past the doors, expecting Bill to come out any second. Bill finally convinced the Inspectors to escort him outside, so that he could tell his wife to go home.

Finally, the Commodore arrived. He was able to convince the Inspectors that Bill was not a mail robber, and Bill was released.

The DevGroup never again went into the mail business.

Guidance

Two fine men – at loggerheads

There are many different foundations for authority. Authority can be formally assigned to a person or a position. It can attach by virtue of age, birthright, or longevity in a position. Authority may be based on a particular ability, technical skill or expertise. It can even be founded on personal charm or charisma. This story relates an incident where three sources of authority were shared among two individuals, and as might be expected, a conflict arose.

In the Naval Service, the authority of a commanding officer[44] is almost absolute. The responsibility for the well-being, safety, and effectiveness of a command extends to every aspect of its operations, and the authority to support that responsibility must be equally sweeping. There are limits, of course, but generally speaking, "the captain's word is law." At sea, his orders and wishes must prevail, and compliance must be unhesitating. In port, the urgency may be less, but the expectation is unchanged. The entire authority structure of a command is essentially an extension of the authority of the commanding officer.

Another authority structure operates in parallel with, and supports, the captain's authority. Submarines for years have had a traditional position known as the "Chief of the Boat". The COB, normally the senior chief petty officer assigned to the ship, is the "captain's right hand" on any policy or activity that affects the enlisted

---

[44] Or of an "officer in charge", if the unit is not formally commissioned.

men of the crew, and that, of course, means virtually everything. In the 1970's, the concept of a senior enlisted man who could carry the crew's concerns up the chain of command and who could help implement directives that came down that same chain, was adopted throughout the Navy. The position of "Master Chief Petty Officer of the Command" (MCPOC) was formalized.[45]

In the third origin of authority for this story, authority is often vested in an individual by virtue of his experience and expertise. Nowhere is this more rigorously demonstrated than in the Navy's designation of a "Master Diver." The "master" is the individual in charge of a dive site, and he is normally in direct communication[46] with the divers on the bottom. He is personally responsible for the divers' safety, and he takes this responsibility very seriously. An order from the master diver is executed immediately and without question.[47] Certification as a "Master Diver" is not conferred lightly.

One of the commands incorporated in Submarine Development Group One was a detachment of Navy divers. This unit maintained one of the Navy's McCann rescue bells[48]. The "Mobile Dive Team" was trained in the air-transport procedures involved in deploying the bell to a remote location, and they would be the personnel who operated the bell during an actual rescue. The Dive Team – about twenty divers

---

[45] Aboard submarines, the MCPOC is still referred to, and will always be, "the COB". The MCPOC is often referred to as the "Command Master Chief".

[46] By electronics, sound-powered telephones, or by a system of "line pull" signals.

[47] For physiologic reasons, divers under pressure may not perceive hazards as clearly as a detached observer, topside. The "rapture of the deep" is not an old wives' tale, but a familiar physiologic phenomenon.

[48] The McCann bell could be lowered and mated to a disabled submarine and used to bring the submarine's crew to the surface

– also honed their diving skills through participation in diving and salvage operations in the San Diego area. It was in this command that the three origins of authority that I have described – formal command, a senior enlisted adviser, and technical expertise – came into conflict.

The Officer in Charge (OinC) of the Mobile Dive Team was a mustang[49] Lieutenant who had been a Navy diver for his entire career. As the command's officer in charge, he was held to the same standards as any skipper. The Navy did not care that he had been a diver, or that he was a mustang. He was in *command* of the Mobile Dive Team, and he was responsible for every aspect of the Team's performance.

The Mobile Dive Team, like every other Navy command, had a formally designated Command Master Chief. He was the senior enlisted man in the command, and like MCPOCs everywhere, he was involved in virtually every aspect of the command's policies and procedures.

Finally, both the OinC and the MCPOC were qualified and certified as Navy Master Divers. There was probably no aspect of diving operations in which these two men were not experts. Theirs is an exceptionally complex field, but they were familiar with every procedure, every requirement, and every piece of diving equipment.

Each of these two men was a well-trained, enthusiastic professional, and each was dedicated to the effectiveness of the command. Unfortunately, they did not get along.

---

[49] The traditional term "mustang" refers to an officer who has been selected from among the enlisted ranks and been given commissioned status. Such an officer often has invaluable experience in a specific technical field, and he is usually assigned where he can best contribute that expertise. My grandfather, Orville Byrd, was a mustang Supply Corps officer.

Neither man was clearly at fault. Neither was "wrong". The two leadership styles were simply different and they were not compatible. The men on the Dive Team could not help but recognize the continuing conflict. To some extent, they were "caught in the middle" and the morale of the team (and its effectiveness) began to suffer. Something had to be done, hopefully without sacrificing the contributions that each of the two senior leaders could offer.

The Navy has several administrative processes to document and to correct deficient performance. One such process is called a "Letter of Instruction", and it is provided to an individual when improved performance is required. In practice, the emphasis is often on documentation of a deficiency, rather than on correction of a problem. It is an admonition, a warning, but it is often couched in such vague euphemisms as to be virtually useless as an instrument of actual improvement.

Nonetheless, it is a severe step. To have received a formal letter of instruction is to have been specifically notified of a deficiency. You have clearly pushed someone too far. A copy of a formal letter of instruction is forwarded to the Bureau of Naval Personnel to be incorporated in an individual's permanent record. If the letter is mentioned in an officer's fitness report (as it should be), it will usually result in non-selection for promotion. If a letter is mentioned in an enlisted evaluation, it will have an equally severe effect. In either case, promotions, awards, special selections, and future assignments are placed in jeopardy.

On a Monday morning, I summoned both the Officer in Charge and the Command Master Chief of the Mobile Dive Team to my office in the Development Group headquarters. They arrived together that afternoon. I presented each of them with an original of the same formal letter of instruction – with a notation that a copy would be submitted to the Bureau of Personnel in Washington. Both men recognized the impact of the letter, and both men were visibly shaken.

In the letter, I presented the fact that the performance of the Mobile Dive Team was being affected by their leaders' inability to work together. I indicated that each had responsibility to support the other, and that each had a valuable perspective. Each had a unique contribution to offer, and each would be well-advised to accept inputs from the other. I refused to take sides, and in a radical departure from the prescribed format for letters of instruction, I presented them no suggestions for improvement.

Rather, I told the two men that *they*, working *together*, would have to come up with a formal improvement program. I wanted them to present a written program to me, with their solution, within ninety-six hours – that is, by Friday afternoon.

On *Wednesday* afternoon, I received a telephone call from the Officer in Charge of the Mobile Dive Team. He and the Command Master Chief had their program. Could they come to see me early? I invited them to come up immediately.

The two men arrived in my office, and offered me the written program they had prepared. I declined it and instead retrieved the official copy of the Letter of Instruction from my desk drawer. I tore the Letter in two and gave each man half, saying "I don't think we need this anymore."

I do not know what program the two men had developed, but I do know that we never again had performance problems with the Mobile Dive Team.